WHILE WAITING OR
WORKING FOR CHANGE...

WHILE WAITING OR WORKING FOR CHANGE...

THINGS TO DO AND PITFALLS TO AVOID IN ERITREA

With Translations in Tigrinya and Arabic

Bereket Habte Selassie

THE RED SEA PRESS
TRENTON | LONDON | NEW DELHI | CAPE TOWN | NAIROBI | ADDIS ABABA | ASMARA | IBADAN

THE RED SEA PRESS
541 West Ingham Avenue | Suite B
Trenton, New Jersey 08638

Book and cover design: Lemlem Taddese

Cataloging-in-Publication data may be obtained from Library of Congress
ISBN: 978-1-56902-414-0 (PB)

TABLE OF CONTENETS

ACKNOWLEDGMENTS

The author would like to thank the translators of the documents in this book, namely: Samuel Bizen (Tigrigna), Abdu Razig (Arabic), and also Tsegu Fissehaie for editing the Tigrigna translation.

Much thanks also goes to Saleh Younis for his kind words in the foreword and Dan Connell for his helpful review and sincere comments.

Finally, I would like to acknowledge my friend and Publisher, Kassahun Checole, for producing this book in record time.

FOREWORD

Salah Yonus

Dr. Bereket Habteselassie's "While Working for Change" reminds one of Lenin's "What Is To Be Done: Burning Questions of Our Movement." In fact, one of the sub-titles in his paper is "What Needs To Be Done." His essay is both diagnostic and prescriptive. Unlike Lenin, who was engaged in scholarly exchange with his peers, Dr. Bereket is (as he has been for over a decade) waging a lone campaign as most Eritrean scholars appear to be completely disengaged from the "burning questions" of our time. It is a point that Dr. Bereket kindly refrains form making even as he proposes workable solution and invites us to stop being observers and become agents for change.

To Dr. Bereket's mind, the "real cause of the crisis in Eritrea" is due to the fact that Isaias Afwerki and the party he controls have completely dominated the country's executive, legislative and judicial arm and have been practicing bad politics and pursuing wrong policies to the point that now Eritrea is "poised between survival and state collapse."

What should be done? Dr. Bereket sees three venues: we keep doing what we have been doing; we admit defeat and surrender to injustice; or find alternates to the way we have been struggling to bring about change. Since the last option is the only option, Dr. Bereket proposes new alternatives: form a united front (as contrasted with unity) with the understanding that nobody needs to be bound by this united front once the objective of bringing about the fall of the regime is accomplished.

This, as Dr. Bereket concedes, has been tried and the paper itemizes all the thorny wedge issues that have made its realization difficult: is our means going to peaceful or armed? Is our relationship with Ethiopia going to be intimate or at arm's length? What is the role of civil societies and political parties? Should we pursue justice or peace and reconciliation? Is the role of the Diaspora to lead the movement or to support and encourage an Eritrea-based movement? Will we use the 1997 constitution as our basis for change or focus on constitutionalism? That is, Dr. Bereket is not offering a blueprint for change as much as crystallizing the choices and making an argument for debate—but only within the context of a united front which he considers of paramount importance. Dr Bereket is saying, as Lenin did, we should step beyond "disunity, dissolution, and vacillation" and approach the existential threat Eritrea faces decisively.

WHILE WAITING OR WORKING FOR CHANGE...

Things to Do and Pitfalls to Avoid

By Bereket Habte Selassie
Distinguished Professor of African Studies and Professor of Law
The University of North Carolina at Chapel Hill
Presented at the Workshop on Eritrea held in Pretoria, May9-11, 2014

First of all, I will lay out the content of my paper. The paper comprises five parts, including the Introduction, which constitutes **Part I**. This is followed by **Part II**, which describes the prevailing condition of our predicament, involving analyses of political, economic and social problems. In **Part III** I point out things that I think must be done in order to resolve the problems described in the preceding part. **Part IV** looks into the future, posing some critical questions and suggesting tentative answers. In **Part V**, the concluding segment of the paper, I take up some controversial issues in a larger, historical perspective and raise the question of the constitution and the role it can play in helping resolve our outstanding issues.

At a time when numerous views are being expressed and proposals made calling for a unity of efforts in the struggle to overthrow the dictatorial regime in Asmara, it occurred to me that toward that end, penning a paper providing a general framework for discussion or debate may be useful; hence this paper.

Introduction

A summary discussion of Eritrea's prevailing condition and its main elements is essential as background for framing the crucial issues confronting us as a nation, particularly in a transitional situation requiring charting out a roadmap for a post-Isaias government. Several Eritrean scholars and activists have been convening meetings, and debating ways of confronting our sad predicament. Lately, we have observed a number of efforts demanding a national consensus on the basic need of unity of efforts. The similarity of sentiments and ideas in all these efforts is striking; so, naturally, one wishes for a combined and coordinated effort to save time and resources—to avoid duplication. My aim in the present paper is to make a modest contribution in helping achieve clarity and coherence and create a unity of efforts in our common objective. In much of the discussion attempted in this paper I adopted the Socratic method of asking questions instead of passing judgments, except where it concerns the constitution and its role as a framework securing mutual recognition as foundation of national existence. Where I venture to suggest solutions to problems, I do so deliberately to set in motion a debate on some controversial issues like crimes committed during the armed struggle.

Some might rightly think that what is needed in the circumstances of our sorry predicament is not a lecture by individuals but an extended conversation among Eritreans. However, perhaps a lecture like this may contribute to a national conversation in search of what needs to be done to secure national consensus on finding a lasting solution. The recent case of many public lectures delivered by one determined and dedicated Eritrean, Tewolde Tesfamariam (Wedi Vaccara), has demonstrated that, when spoken from the heart and with passion, a speech by one individual can have an impact on the wider community of Eritreans. Lately, after several of Tewolde's speeches, some people have asked: what next? Where does this lead us in terms of concrete action? These are good questions, and that brings me to the topic of my own address—what has to be done concretely to bring about the needed change.

The theme of the Pretoria workshop covers several issues concerning Eritrea's problems. For convenience of presentation I propose to bundle the themes generally under political, economic and social headings. So I will proceed accordingly, beginning with a narrative of the basic elements of our country's predicament, viewed in historical perspective. Discussions on Eritrean issues, especially concerning the history of the Ghedli, invariably involve competitive narratives more or less reflecting differing perspectives of the two historic organizations, the ELF and the EPLF. Recently, there have been some encouraging signs of reconciliation of the competing narratives. In the face of the common aim confronting a common adversary such new development is indeed encouraging.

The Prevailing Condition and Its Elements

It has become trite to observe that twenty years after its liberation from Ethiopian occupation, Eritrea finds itself at a critical juncture, standing perilously poised between survival and state collapse. The Lampedusa tragedy represents a historic moment that compels all of us to face the bitter truth. The truth is that Eritrea's youth--the guarantor of the nation's future—is in danger of losing hope for the future; and a nation without a hopeful youth has no future. Eritrea's government, which had begun with a promise to bring about democracy, prosperity, and the rule of law, has become instead the cause of endless conflict and the consequent suffering and despair of its people. The government of Isaias Afwerki and his party, People's Front for Democracy and Justice (PFDJ) have brought to the people neither democracy nor justice. Indeed, they have broken a solemn promise and squandered scarce resources and golden opportunities by being engaged in dangerous politics and pursuing ruinous policies. In adopting what they call a national service, which in actual fact is forcible servitude, they have pinned down a whole generation of Eritrean youth in the wilderness wasting their lives and depriving their aging parents the support and succor they need in their golden years. It was after escaping the unending servitude that the youth drowned at Lampedusa. Others had also previously drowned in the Mediterranean Sea though in smaller numbers.

Let me summarize the grim reality that has been the lot of Eritreans as dramatized by the Lampedusa tragedy.

- There is a continuing violation of basic human rights—rights guaranteed under the 1997 ratified constitution as well as under all rules and norms of international law.
- The country is ruled by executive directives issuing out of the office of an unelected president. Such directives are not subject to any review and override all notions of the rule of law.
- The governing party (PFDJ) has virtual monopoly of all business through its mammoth economic apparatus, the Red Sea Corporation and its several affiliates.
- The militarization of society has resulted in a brutalized captive population. Every person between the ages of 18 and 50 (for males) and between 18 and 40 (for females) is subject to military service that has no time limit.
- As a result of these conditions, there has been social and economic dislocation, including the disruption of educational and career opportunities of an entire generation of Eritreans.
- Above all, the promise of democratic transition to a constitutional government has been denied in favor of

one party—one man—rule. All this is in violation of the resolutions of two congresses of the ruling party and the provisions of the 1997 constitution. This violation is the real cause of the crisis in Eritrea.

Elements of the Crisis

Politics of Domination and Exclusion

As already noted, the government is based on the monopoly of power held by a single party led by its chairman, President Isaias Afwerki. Though there is a nominal division of government in three branches of legislative, executive and judicial branches, in fact the executive headed by Isaias, dominates the entire government making a mockery of the idea of the rule of law and separation of powers. Everything is centralized with a tight short leash held by one man assisted by a cabal of party hacks. And such local administration as exists is an extension of the central power, organized along six provincial areas nominally headed by administrators appointed by the president. However, since 2002, the administrators have been required by presidential decree to report to military overseers (commanding generals of the regional armies) who in turn report to the president. This condition has enhanced the militarization of government and society and deepened the sense of helplessness of civil society, which is intimidated into silence.

One way of expressing the principal problem of politics in Eritrea is to say that there is complete absence of government accountability and transparency. It was thus that in 1998 an irresponsible president started a war with Ethiopia without consulting the cabinet or the National Assembly. Things came to a head when, following the disastrous war some prominent members of the party and government challenged the president to be held accountable. To that end, they asked for a meeting of the party's top institution and of the National Assembly to review the decision that took the country to war resulting in the occupation of a sizable portion of Eritrean land by Ethiopian troops. In a word, a group of people who had been his comrades-in-arms of the liberation war and colleagues in the government whom he had dominated for years, since then known as G-15, challenged Isaias for the first time. They sought to hold him accountable for starting a war without consulting them and the National Assembly. His response was arrogant refusal to do what they asked, coupled with a threat of dire consequences to them if they persisted in what they started.

Then, in the wake of the September 11, 2001 terrorist attack on America, when the attention of the world was distracted, Isaias ordered the arrest of 11 members of G-15. He also ordered the arrest of the editors and reporters of the newly formed independent press that had also posed a challenge by writing critical articles and publishing interviews of some members of G-15. The arrest of 11 members of G-15 and of journalists galvanized Eritrean public opinion particularly among the Diaspora communities. New political parties emerged opposing the government as well as civic organizations that demanded accountability of the government for human rights violations and demanding the implementation of the 1997 constitution. For, contrary to the hopes and expectations of many thoughtful people, what Isaias did in response to the demands of the G-15 and other members of the Eritrean public went beyond all expectations. The president did indeed convene a National Assembly, but not to fulfill the request of the G-15; instead, he submitted a proposal to the captive assembly charging the G-15 with treason and other crimes. The assembly dutifully passed a resolution approving the proposal. On September 18, 2001, 11 members of the G-25 were arrested and held incommunicado in an unknown prison. [Three members of the G-15 happened to be abroad escaping imprisonment and later became part of the resistance movement].

As we can see, we have an obedient National Assembly at the beck and call of the president. What about the judiciary? A promising start at institution building had been made with the ratification of the 1997 constitution, which guaranteed an independent judiciary. The Chief Justice of the Supreme Court sought to give life and force to that guarantee by acting independently of the executive. In an international conference held in Asmara, he spoke about executive interference, openly criticizing the president of executive interference in the conduct of judicial process.

For the record, no one among the attendees of the conference uttered a word of support, or asked questions or made any comment regarding the speech of the Chief Justice. Evidently, the intimidation-induced silence affected not only Eritreans but also foreign friends of Eritrea who took part in the conference.

Within days, the Chief Justice was summarily dismissed by the president. Needless to say, as head of state and commander-in-chief of the armed forces, the president controls all aspects of the military and associated security services, and thus presides over a militarized society. In a word he is a dictator whose word is law.

Economics of State Monopoly and Deprivation

Eritrea's economy is in utter shambles. The slogan of self-reliance, which had served a useful purpose during the armed struggle, has not only outlived its usefulness; it has become a straight-jacket from which the economy cannot extract itself. Moreover, the "command economy" inherited from the Ethiopian government (Dergue) has not been abandoned by the PFDJ, which is itself principally led by recovering Marxist-Leninist ideologues. Private enterprise which had been promised under a "mixed economy" has not been encouraged—far from it. The government's vaunted idea of a Singapore-style development project has failed. To begin with, the conditions that vaulted Singapore to a first class economy do not apply to Eritrea. Eritrea's economy—agriculture, livestock, light industry—does not provide a sufficient base for a "takeoff." The hopes pinned on marine resources, minerals, and tourism, which were expected to draw foreign investment and provide employment, have been shattered on the rock of wrong policies and disastrous politics, and consequently could not attract the expected investment.

The government proclaimed its priority of human resources development, presumably influenced by the Singapore model. To that end, it redefined administrative policies and seemed to promise a great deal. This objective was later denied by the militarization of society and allocation of a lion's share of budget resources to the security sector, leaving education and other social services at a huge disadvantage. Moreover, there has been no rational and publicly debated policy on education, including higher education. The only university of the nation was steadily degraded and eventually abolished in favor of "Technical colleges" that have been opened in a few places and are headed by military officers. Students of these hybrid institutions are spared the obligatory "national service," but they are subject to recall at any time. The government considers this project of unpaid human labor as a short-cut toward achieving economic development. However the result has not confirmed the proclaimed aims. Indeed, it has been a waste of human resources and the cause of human suffering and social dislocation as already noted.

In sum, judging by the economic performance of the last few years, the outlook appears bleak, if not downright dismal. Growth measured by GDP is expected to remain below 2 percent, even with the revenue coming out of the mining sector. The main source of growth, such as it is, has been donor-funded projects and remittances from abroad (i.e. from Eritreans in the Diaspora). Hence the government's dogged insistence on imposing a 2 per cent tax on all Eritreans in the Diaspora as a condition of giving them permits due to a citizen to perform all kinds of social and human services such as weddings, funerals and related matters that citizens expect from a legitimate government. The impact of this economy of deprivation is clearly seen in people's lives.

A Landscape of Social Decay

A country's social condition is naturally impacted by worsening economic conditions and political crisis. This has been the case in Eritrea for over a decade, with the situation worsening following the 1998-2000 war with Ethiopia. Even before the onset of that devastating war, the policy and politics of domination and exclusion—political domination by the PFDJ, excluding other political parties as well as the monopolization of the economy practiced by the government—had foreshadowed the current social crisis. Judged by the standard of the United Nation's Human Development Index (HDI), Eritrea is ranked very low. Eritrea's HDI in the year 2004 for example was 0.45 putting it as number 157 out of 177 countries—right at the bottom, trailing behind 156 countries. (See UNDP HDI Report, 2006).

The Human Development Index is a useful measure of human wellbeing, going beyond Gross Domestic Product (GDP). It embraces different dimensions of human development, most importantly: the availability of affordable and adequate nutrition; provision of affordable education; access to good health services and affordable housing in safe neighborhoods. Eritrea's extremely low HDI score in the 2006 survey demonstrates, beyond question, failure in the provision of these services to the majority of the population. A proud and hardworking people have been reduced to the condition of a beggar nation, dependent on the generosity of external donors for their survival in matters as basic as food. Though drought has exacerbated their predicament, today as before, the cause of the Eritrean people's distress cannot be blamed on Nature alone. Wrong policies and politics are the real culprits. It is indeed paradoxical that a government that proclaims its abhorrence of dependence on outsiders has steadily become dependent on outside aid, even as it denies international nongovernmental organizations' (NGO) role in the provision of basic needs.

A tragic dimension of the social crisis in Eritrea concerns the plight of the elderly who have been left to fend for themselves at a time in their lives when their children were expected to look after them—and would have looked after them. Scores of thousands of Eritrean youth have been pinned down in the trenches in the desert on "national service" wasting their youth, foregoing education or raising children, leaving their parents to penury and lonely old age. Thousands of our youth have escaped to neighboring countries and beyond as the Lampedusa tragedy demonstrated. Others who could not or would not dare to escape continue to live as condemned prisoners in servitude.

The shops in the cities and towns may be stocked with imported goods, but the sight of long bread lines has become common. People line up starting at 5 am and may wait for hours only to be told there is no more bread—come tomorrow. The overcrowded schools do not have sufficient books and other educational materials, and teachers are paid salaries that cannot carry them to the end of the month. The health services are so poor that the few lucky ones who can afford it travel abroad for medical treatment—this in a nation that boasted of miraculous health services in the valley of the "liberated areas" during the liberation struggle.

In view of this disheartening reality, one wonders how patriotic and duty-minded Eritreans in the government have coped in the circumstances. The answer is that they do their best to meet the challenge of a worsening condition of their people. But their best efforts fall short of what is required simply because they operate in a reality defined by bad policies and politics over which they have no control. Any attempt to question the policies or to make critical comments result in harsh treatment and the fate of G-15 and the imprisoned journalists serves as a warning, with an expanded and ubiquitous security monitoring people's words and actions. "Big Brother" is watching everybody all the time.

Nothing can be done domestically; so all eyes have turned to Eritreans in the Diaspora whose number has increased tenfold over the last decade.

What Needs to Be Done

In the context of the political, economic and social crisis described above, the question in everyone's mind is what is to be done. What has to be done: a) to change this tragic situation, and b) to avoid pitfalls or repeat the mistakes of the past?

Any attempt at answering this question must begin with the dire need of unity. On January 11, 2009, I was invited to deliver the keynote address at the founding Conference of CDRiE (Citizens for Democratic Rights in Eritrea), held in London, UK. On that occasion, I congratulated the conference conveners for their initiative. I told them that I considered the founding of their organization as one of the milestones in the struggle of Eritreans to advance the cause of democracy and the rule of law in our benighted country. Noting the emergence of several civic society organizations with objectives similar to those of CDRiE, I said that this is part of a very encouraging trend that gives hope to a generally disheartened Eritrean Diaspora community.

The title of my keynote address was "Unity for the Greater Good: Reflections of an Elder on His Nation's Predicament." My paper, I told my audience, represented the thinking of a man who is transitioning to a less active and more reflective phase of his life and career. My remarks came as a surprise to some of the members of the audience (who apparently thought I was ageless!), especially when I said, "…As I traverse through my septuagenarian years, I am conscious of the rush of time, and of the fact that there remain some unfinished business that I devoutly wish should be finished, and would like to devote a significant part of what remains of my life to help accomplish…" One such unfinished business, I said, is the continuing division among Eritreans, while a ruthless dictator rules over our people bringing the nation to the brink of ruin.

Five years have elapsed since that speech, and we remain as divided as ever.

What continues to be a source of confusion and endless dispute is the question of how to resolve the problems of our nation—how to bring about change and thus rescue a long-suffering people from the clutches of a tyrannical regime. It bears repetition that if the prevailing crisis in our country remains unaddressed it might result in a catastrophic end—the end of the nation as we know it. That possibility should focus our minds to search for a timely solution. The first thing we need to demand is a united front to change the regime of Isaias Afwerki and his PFDJ to usher in a democratic system. Many thoughtful Eritreans in the Diaspora have undertaken vigorous efforts aimed at the creation or consolidation of a united front. Everyone seems to be convinced of the necessity of such a united front in the conviction that we should not remain a divided community while a ruthless dictator and his henchmen destroy our nation.

The First of Two Agendas

In the attempt at the unification of our efforts, we need to agree on two separate, but related, agendas. One is the consolidation of a united front dedicated to changing the regime. The other is the preservation and refinement of the different parties that have emerged with a view to encouraging multi-party democracy in a post-Isaias democratic system. As we consider the first agenda, we should always be aware of the pitfalls. In view of the tendency of the different groups—both political parties and civic rights organizations—to be engaged in a zero-sum game can we proceed on the assumption that they will be amenable to the idea of a united front based on a common aim of regime change? My own view is that most of them will be. It is certainly worthwhile to try our best to get them to agree, rather than wait for change to happen providentially!

To that end the example of CDRiE provides a useful lesson. At the time of my keynote address and thereafter, I asked the question whether CDRiE can act as a *unifying force* among Eritreans who remain dispersed along several axes of division. Five years after, I have seen no evidence indicating a positive answer to that question. Nor is this peculiar to CDRiE; in many respects, the same applies to other civic organizations like EGS (Eritrean Global Solidarity). There may be other civic organizations with similar aims as those of CDRiE and EGS of which I am not aware. One could reasonably assume, as I did in 2009, that the leaders of these civic organizations possess the requisite commitment, resilience and wisdom to navigate the rough waters of contemporary Eritrean social and political reality.

Experience of the recent past has shown the tendency of Eritrean organizations, both political and civic, to split and create more organizations. In the context of the yet unfulfilled promise of unity, this tendency has confused and frustrated Eritreans everywhere. A historical perspective always helps to explain this phenomenon of splits. As mentioned before, there was a ray of hope in the late 1990's and early 2000, following the demand by the G-15 for democratic transformation. With the creation of new parties and revival of ELF-based factions the hope of change and renewal was revived. Eritreans in general and members of the various parties demanded unity of the parties and factions. Consequently, after years of tortuous negotiations among the various factions, the Eritrean Democratic Alliance (EDA) eventually emerged and convened conferences in pursuit of a larger unity transcending religious, ethnic and factional differences. The last significant meeting held in Awassa, Ethiopia, established the *Baito* and the pursuit of national unity and consensus on major issues continues to this day. Meanwhile the EPLF-based EDP joined the former ELF-RC to form Eritrean People's Democratic Party (EPDP), apparently having resolved what I have called their competing narratives on the history of the division.

The Second Agenda: Unity and Diversity

In proclaiming the primacy of national unity, which is a legitimate assertion, some people nonetheless worry that in the process of fulfilling that critical requirement for success in the struggle to change the current regime, we may unintentionally ensure the installation of the same centralized authoritarian government that is the cause of our present condition. This is a legitimate concern, given the history of regime change that went awry as has been seen in Egypt following the "Arab Spring." The answer to this legitimate concern is that a general agreement must be reached that the parties and factions that are to be united for the purpose of regime change can conceivably go their separate ways as different political organizations to be part of a new era of healthy diversity and multi-party democracy. This is needed in order to guarantee against the return of an authoritarian government. There must be a clear agreement on this point, an agreement that may incidentally help in persuading some reluctant people to be part of the united front designed to ensure effective regime change. It is my fervent hope that the many newly-minted party formations will do the job of leading a vigorous united political opposition to score victory against an entrenched, ruthless regime that has political, financial and diplomatic assets at its disposal.

Admittedly, the prospect of success is set against some difficult challenges ahead. One such challenge is the rapprochement between the PFDJ government and the government of Sudan, which has dealt a serious blow to the opposition. As a result, some Eritrean escapees were forcibly repatriated, and the offices of the opposition in Khartoum were closed. It has forced all opposition parties, including those that had previously resisted, to open offices in Addis Ababa. In the jaded eyes of pragmatic observers this political expediency is seen favorably, while those Eritreans who blame the "Weyane" for many things and are suspicious of its future ambitions (The Greater Tigray hypothesis) reacted negatively to the opening of offices in Addis Ababa. The division among Eritreans on this issue is a reflection of the growing complexity of Eritrean politics, and the politics of the region. A further complication of the situation is caused by the post-Badme war reality, a condition of no-peace-no-war stalemate in which Ethiopia continues to occupy a part of Eritrean territory.

The Continuing Search for a Way Out

So what is to be done? The generally favored option is to continue calling for the overthrow of Isaias's regime and demand his trial for various crimes. Many have been doing that for some years now, as members of political parties as well as in their individual capacities. All in vain. An essential part of this option concerns controversy over the modality of bringing about regime change—through peaceful means, or through armed struggle. For a people who have spent two generations in armed struggle and paid a heavy price in blood and treasure, most Eritreans are reluctant to accept the option of armed struggle, When challenged by the protagonists of armed struggle to explain how they propose to attain their objective through peaceful means, they respond that organizing people inside Eritrea, by all .means possible is a must. Secondly, they stress diplomacy particularly seeking assistance from neighboring countries, especially Ethiopia.

On this point of contention there has been an ongoing debate among the opposition political parties whose outcome is inconclusive. The different opposition political parties have not as yet agreed on a common diplomatic strategy, and the various civic organization and some leaders of the Internet websites have made attempts to force the issues through interviews and articles posted in their respective websites. It is my sense that the vast majority of Eritreans prefer the peaceful option, though some prefer to leave it open by adding that the option of the use of military means should not be foreclosed. Assuming that the peaceful means is the one preferred by the majority of Eritreans, it would be incumbent upon all concerned to insist on a common diplomatic strategy as well as a front to mobilize and organize Eritreans inside the country. The radio broadcast begun by the MedreK group is very promising and it can be used as the nucleus of a coordinated campaign just as the initiative of Wedi Vaccaro can be a center of a massive popular organization to push the campaign for change homeward to which other initiatives can be coalesced. What we do not need is unsavory competition among these opposition forces.

Guilt, Redemption and Rectification

Apart from the options noted above, another option is the avenue of national reconciliation. We need to be clear as to what is at stake in this connection? My recent research that led to the publication of Wounded Nation showed me that there were some unpleasant aspects about the armed struggle—much tawdry and revolting stuff amid noble deeds and extraordinary acts of heroism. Our nation has a great need of healing from the psychic wounds inflicted upon it in a long armed struggle. Such healing must begin first of all with acceptance of the fact that we are part of a wounded nation. We need all the help we can muster in a long process of healing. But admission of the fact of wounding is an essential precondition. Such admission is also a precondition for national reconciliation. Some may argue that it is the other way round: that national healing can only happen in consequence of national reconciliation. The question is: can there be such a reconciliation that leaves out the issue of Isaias's culpability for his historic crimes? Nor is Isaias the only culprit. Considering the difficulty surrounding this issue, most people with whom I discussed this issue express the view that the issue of charging Isaias can only be addressed following the end of his regime and the establishment of a democratic, constitutional government. Which becomes a vicious circle.

Aside from the question of criminal charge and guilt, almost all the opposition parties have mapped out solutions under which they prescribe for the ailing Eritrean body politic democratic change and the installation of constitutional government with the rule of law and human rights as the core of the system. Most would agree with the prescriptions, but needless to say, the real question is: how are these prescriptions to be put into effect? In answering this question, at the risk of repetition, we need to be clear about one thing—there can be no change without a movement inside Eritrea.

Clearly, in view of the total denial of freedom of speech and organization, and the oppressive security apparatus that has a stranglehold on a terrorized Eritrean population, the emergence of a movement from within is difficult if not impossible. The "Forto" attempt by Wedi Ali demonstrated that there is, simmering below the surface, an unorganized movement that can and should be probed and organized. In sum, a coordinated, national opposition movement inside Eritrea needs encouragement and support from Eritreans in the Diaspora. How this can be done is the main question of the day.

At this point, it is pertinent to mention the recent appearance of group of some young Eritrean scholars who seem to think that change can come from within, not by seeking to overthrow the regime, but by appealing to the top leadership of the Eritrean government and its party to effect change themselves. To that end, they wrote a letter addressed to all the members of the top echelon of the government, notably members of the Cabinet and top party leaders. Written in the wake of the Lampedusa disaster, the letter is couched in diplomatic respectful language and was clearly based on the assumption that the addressees of the letter shared the democratic values of the writers of the letter. It certainly does not seem to share the view of most Eritreans in the opposition regarding the crimes Isaias is accused of having committed during the armed struggle. Even taking a sanguine view of the scholars and respecting their right to hold views favorable to Isaias and his regime, their assumption that Isaias would respond to an appeal to "mend his ways" is naïve to say the least. On the other side, the case for holding Isaias answerable for his crimes and bringing him to face justice has been advanced in meetings and in articles posted in opposition websites. Recently, one scholar, a political science professor, has presented a paper at an EGS sponsored meeting in Washington DC. The initiative of the scholar concerned seems to be to start a mass movement demanding that Isaias face criminal justice.

The Diaspora and the Refugee Issue

Meanwhile, there are some urgent problems that the Diaspora opposition needs to address, problems facing Eritreans in the countries of their refuge in Europe, America and elsewhere. Recently, I shared some of the following notes with a few Eritrean compatriots, seeking their thoughts about how we can together help provide some answers to these questions, and related problems, facing our country.

I framed the issues under a heading in the form of a question—*Which Way Eritrea.* In asking the questions and offering my own suggestions, I want to make it clear that I do not represent any party or group; but I do declare that Eritrean opposition parties have my sincere support in what they are trying to accomplish, as do all civic organizations. At the same time, I fervently hope that all opposition organizations will discard the legacy of bitter strife and become united in a new spirit of patriotic duty to save the nation. They have to think afresh, and creatively work out a viable and united opposition. Only in such spirit and unity can they lead us to victory against PFDJ's tyrannical rule. It is a conclusion that I reached having observed opposition politics over the past ten years and analyzed the available evidence concerning their activities. Though some progress has been made toward unification of efforts, it falls far short of what is required to attain the goal of democratic change in Eritrea.

Civic society organizations have emerged in America and Europe with some dedicated individual Eritreans playing positive roles. But considering the need for regime change, civic organizations, important though they are, should not be expected to replace effective political party work. There should be general agreement that where the roles of the two might coincide, civic society organizations can at best be supplementary to, not substitutive of, political parties. One can imagine situations under which it may be morally compelling for civic organizations to condemn certain acts or omissions of governments or organizations, where political organizations may find it diplomatically not wise to do so, but might quietly support the condemnation concerned. In any case, civic society organizations too need to be more united and better structured in order to perform their tasks. That was why I accepted the invitation to take part in the founding conference of CDRiE without the slightest hesitation. In the same spirit I also attended meetings convened by EGS. Indeed, I have been privileged to be given a certificate of recognition by EGS as "The Voice of Rule of Law," an honor for which I am deeply grateful.

It is worth emphasizing, however, that civic organizations need clarity and coherence in their goals and objectives, clearly demarcating their role from those of political opposition parties in order to avoid misunderstanding and unnecessary conflict. Both political parties and civic society organizations are expected to play a role in exposing the outrage being committed by the PFDJ regime against our people, and to help provide remedies to some of the victims, especially those who escape from its clutches. In this task, the opposition Internet Websites have a crucial role to play. In their case also, there has to be clarity and a basic agreement on their common objective and avoid unnecessary confrontations and mutual recrimination. One of their key common objectives is draw the vast army of refugees to their ranks and mobilize them for the needed change. Clearly, this is an issue on which everyone needs to recognize that their efforts have fallen short of what is required. In order to succeed, opposition organizations need to redouble their efforts and be creative in drawing to their ranks more and more of the vast army of young Eritrean refugees escaping from the clutches of the regime. To that end, it is important to analyze the composition of the Diaspora.

The vast majority of the members of the Diaspora are the escapees of the last ten years Their epic story of escape is testimonial to the human spirit—to courage, determination, persistence and ingenuity—a characteristic that defines Eritreans. A few of these heroic escapees have joined one or more of the political parties; some have joined the civic organizations. The vast majority remain outside of the groups, tending to go with the flow and concerned with daily problems of survival, and wishing to forget the harsh life that they left behind. Many indeed express extreme sentiments about their experience and do not want to be reminded of it, or even of Eritrea. They boldly assert that they have amply paid their dues and tell recruiters of political parties or civic organizations to spare them preaching about nation and people, which to them sounds utterly sanctimonious. They are bitter and it is anybody's guess as to whether they can be eventually induced to recover their faith in the nation that they left behind. Many seem to see their future in their adopted country of refuge, not in the nation they left behind. This is indeed one of the saddest aspects of the current Eritrean reality. It raises some serious questions with deeper implications for Eritrea's future.

"This too Shall Pass"

Since the Lampedusa tragedy, the question of the massive exodus of Eritrean youth from their homeland to various foreign countries, mostly Europe and North America, has become a subject deserving more serious attention than it received so far. Such attention is divided between the short-term view of procuring help to the refugees who are in urgent need of different kinds, and the mid-to-long term view. In the long term the subject can be a topic for serious research by students of politics, sociology or history. But that is a luxury that those with urgent need cannot even contemplate. During my research conducted in 2009-2010, I was informed by members of the evangelical churches that some four thousand of the escapees (which I called the Sawa Refugees) have joined their churches. I have a feeling that theirs is a growing number, and the evangelical Christians seem to be motivated to lead a purposeful life—study, get a good job and raise families—and are better placed to receive assistance from their fellow evangelicals in the countries of their refuge, the United Kingdom being a good example. In my opinion the opposition, especially the civic segment, needs to consider these Eritreans with all the seriousness they deserve and involve them in their constructive activities. The guiding principle is that all Eritreans must be part of all decisions affecting their destiny as a people without any distinction based on religion, region or ethnicity.

When I think of the plight of Eritreans in our time I cannot help remembering the haunting words of the victims of the

Sinai Bedowin. The words uttered by some of our young compatriots who were tortured before their kidneys were harvested in the Sinai Peninsula are unforgettable. Even in the face of death, while their vital organs were being cut out of their bodies they left for posterity the words, **"This too shall pass.**" Anyone who doubts the indomitable spirit of Eritreans in crisis needs to remember these unsung heroes. An all of us should find in the spirit of those heroic young Eritreans something to inspire us to persevere.

We need to think hard and focus clearly upon the dire needs of our suffering compatriots and discuss what should be done to alleviate their suffering and help provide a solution. What can be done to help them cope, survive and become contributors to the common cause? Since providing aid and comfort to Eritrean refugees is of prime importance, opposition civil societies need to look for different sources of support—official and unofficial—for Eritrean refugees. The task forces that have been initiated by different groups of Eritreans beginning in 2008 is a good initiative. The commendable initiative Wedi Vaccaro has taken should be transformed into a campaign for both political change and civic initiatives to help Eritrean refugees and displaced persons everywhere. The most urgent attention must be turned to the plight of Eritrean refugees in Israel and the Sinai region of Egypt where horrible crimes have been, and are being committed.

Mutual Recognition—the First Principle of National Existence

Looking into the future of a post-Isaias Eritrea, and considering our predicament, as described in the foregoing sections, we have to ask some crucial questions regarding our reality and how to manage and/or transform the reality. But first, we start with the constitutional proposition that a nation comprising diverse communities *must accept mutual recognition as the governing principle of national existence.* Whatever type of constitution we adopt, we cannot omit this first principle. An eminent Canadian scholar has expressed it thus: "The question of our age …is whether a constitution can give recognition to the legitimate demands of the members of diverse cultures in a manner that renders everyone their due, so that all would freely consent to this form of constitutional association. Let us call this 'mutual recognition' and ask what it entails." (James Tully).

With respect to this matter, we need to ask whether we see fault-lines underlying the diversity of the nation. If so, are such fault-lines bridgeable, and what must political organizations do in that regard in order to address them for the preservation of Eritrea as an integrated nation state? Do religious and ethnic divides constitute such fault-lines?

If so, what must be done to bridge the gap underlying the divide? What lessons can we learn from the past particularly with respect to the religious divide, and what constitutional provisions must we insist upon to that end? Have any of the existing Eritrean political and civic organizations addressed this issue? If so, in what way, and with what result? There have been serious expressions or manifestations of the existence of such fault lines, invariably expressed in terms of exclusion of some communities from governance and the allocation of resources. Is the emergence of different political organizations a negative or positive sign of the fault-lines? Can their emergence be subsumed under the principle of unity-in-diversity?

I start with the assumption that all the different groups, including the recently formed groups like MedreK and similar organizations have the best interest of their country and people at heart, and that they can help in building bridges across the divide. I also assume that only bridge building offers a solution to the persistence of division in our nation. Nor does this apply to organizations only; it should apply to individuals such as the extraordinary phenomenon that is Wedi Vaccaro, who seems to have touched the hearts of most Eritreans in the Diaspora, judging by the multitudes that throng to his meetings and his untiring efforts to promote a united front to challenge the dictatorial regime in Asmara. I this respect, the last thing we need is a fallout of mutual recrimination and turf fights among the emerging groups. We need all groups, and we need them to be united to advance the common objective leaving aside any narrowly-based personal or sectarian interest. Once the aim of regime change is achieved, we can all say: Let a hundred schools of thought contend; let there be a multiplicity of parties.

More Questions to All Eritreans

1. What are your thoughts on the conditions described above in this paper, the tragic scenario of suffering Eritreans?
2. What do you think Eritreans in the Diaspora should do?
3. Given Isaias's motive for creating the Sawa "National Service," namely to control the youth and thus maintain himself in power, do you think the PFDJ regime will change its policy on Sawa, as some Eritreans seem to think?
4. Since the vast majority of the Eritreans in the Diaspora have chosen to remain outside the opposition camp, and since the opposition has not demonstrated ability to change either the regime or to cause change in its policy and politics, what should we do now?

Possible scenarios

In view of the reality of a regime wedded to doing whatever it likes, to the detriment of people's interest, consider the following alternatives for people to adopt:

(a) Continue as before?
(b) Admit defeat and submit to the PFDJ and forget all idea of struggle?
(c) Find an alternative framework of struggle?

I cannot imagine anyone, other than the PFDJ supporters, recommending (a) and (b). So, would you agree that the answer is (c)? If that is the answer, the question becomes what kind of framework and what do we do with the existing organizations?

Clearly, it would be neither desirable, no feasible to advocate doing away with the present opposition camp. It is not desirable because it is a ready-made political and social capital that has a history and in which people have invested much in terms of life-time service and dedication. It is not feasible because, human nature being what it is, it is impossible to persuade people who have invested in the political parties and civic organizations to abandon their respective parties or organizations. Indeed, it would be counter-productive to do so. So then what is to be done?

Conclusion

I will conclude by revisiting two issues of concern. One is the need to agree on a constitution; the other is the issue of crime and punishment.

With respect to the constitution, my views are generally known. I strongly believe as did Wedi Ali and his comrades, that the 1997 constitution should be used as a common ground for changing the Isaias regime. Then a new convention can review it with a view to amending parts of it or even adopting a new constitution. With regard to the second issue some (perhaps most) Eritreans seem to insist on punishment for past crimes of the Eritrean leaders, while others believe in forgiveness for the sake of national unity and peace? The latter contend that in order to achieve national reconciliation it is sometimes necessary to decide to let bygones be bygones, forgive past crimes committed during the armed struggle. Eritreans who might have been victims of ELF and EPLF leaders during the struggle, or who are relatives of victims, may need a lot of convincing to accept the idea of forgiveness even for the sake of a reconciled and united country. It may be a bitter pill to swallow; but we need to think hard and consider the alternative. We need to think of the Greater Good. We need an extensive national debate. This happens to lie in my area of professional interest; and I have conducted research on the subject of crime and punishment with respect to some African countries, including: South Africa, Uganda, Sierra Leone and Liberia.

There are two seemingly opposed imperatives involved. One is the imperative of reconciliation and peace. The other is the imperative of justice. Justice demands that offenders be brought to face a tribunal and receive appropriate punishment for crimes they committed. The victims or the relatives of deceased victims naturally support a demand that the offenders face justice. This is natural and to be expected. On the other hand, in the face of unending conflict as in some African countries, or unending tyranny as in our own case, **we may be faced with a historic necessity of compromise**. The South Africans did it by establishing a **Truth and Reconciliation Commission** under which offenders were given a choice to appear before a Commission and confess their offences and ask for forgiveness. Those who refused to confess were charged and prosecuted.

Under the present condition, we Eritreans in the opposition may not be able to emulate the South African model of resolving issues of crime and punishment. For one thing, there has to be a government in place to create such a commission and mandate its authority to deal with the matter. We do not have such a government, unless, of course, Isaias can be persuaded to agree to do so, on the basis of a general amnesty granted to him and to everyone else implicated in past crimes. Many in the opposition may be opposed to amnesty for past crimes.

Finally, we have a fallback position; and that is our social capital, both modern and traditional. Our modern social capital comprises poets and professional people who have been sidelined for far too long in the course of our struggle. On the traditional side, we have elders, and religious leaders some of whom may also be poets or professionals. A revival of traditional social capital is something of value in and of itself; and such revival can be triggered by our current need for reconciliation and restitution. We need seriously to consider making a roster of Eritrean elders, including civic and religious leaders who are among us in the Diaspora, as well as our poets and professional people. Such a roster should include names of people from both civic and political organizations. Every one of the elders must surely have names of people inside Eritrea whom they can contact discretely and mobilize them secretly, at first.

All these remarks and the suggestions that I have made in this paper stem from the profound sense of urgency that I feel and my firm belief that we have to consider them seriously if our nation is to survive. I hope they will get the attention they deserve at this conference and beyond. The urgency is conditioned by a sense of an impending danger—of the possibility of losing forever a once promising nation. I address this urgent call especially to the members of the millennial generation and those immediately above them in age that were in their teens when our nation was born out of the white heat of armed struggle. Will you, and we your elders, remain as mere observers while our nation gradually disintegrates or will you become its saviors?

ቀዳሚ ቃል

ሳልሕ ዮኑስ

ናይ ዶክተር በረኸት ሃብተስላሴ "ኣብ መስርሕ ቃልሳዊ ጉዕዞ" እትብል ጽሕፍቲ፡ ንናይ ለኒን "እንታይ ክግበር ኣለዎ (ኣገደስቲ ሕቶታት ምንቅስቓስና)" እትብል ጽሕፍቲ እያ እተዘኻኽር። ሓንቲ ካብተን ንኡሳን ኣርእስታ 'ውን "እንታይ ክግበር ኣለዎ" እያ ትብል። እዛ ጽሕፍቲ ምርምራዊትን ኣማቲትን እያ። ዶክተር በረኸት ካብ ለኒን ዝፈልዮ ኩነታት እንተ ሃልዩ፡ ለኒን ምስ ማሓዙቱ ስነሓሳባዊ ምልውዋጥ ከካይድ ከሎ፡ ንሱ ግን ንበይኑ ንልዕሊ ዓሰርተ ዓመታት፡ መብዛሕትኦም ምሁራት ኤርትራውያን ካብ 'ዚ ተሃዋሲ እዋናዊ ሕቶታት ኣግሊሎም ኣብ ዘለዉሉ እዋን፡ ናይ ግዜና ኣገደስቲ ሕቶታት እናልዓለ ይገጥሞ ኣሎ። ነዚ ጽሑፍ ፍሉይ ዝገብሮ፡ ዶክተር በረኸት ናይ ኣመራርሓ ውዱእ ቅዲ ክህበና ኣይመረጸን። ክስርሓሎም ዘለዎም መፍትሒታት ብምጥቃስ 'ዩ ንኩላትና ካብ ናይ ተዓዛብነት ቦታ ወጺእና፡ ናይ ለውጢ ሃዋርያታት ንኸንከውን ዓዲሙና።

ብኣረኣእያ ዶክተር በረኸት፡ "እቲ ናይ 'ዚ ሕጂ ኣብ ኤርትራ ተፈጢሩ ዘሎ ቅልውላው ቀንዲ ጠንቂ"፡ ኢሳይያስ ኣፍወርቂ ብመንገዲ እታ ንሱ ዝመርሓ ሰልፊ ኣቢሉ ነቲ ናይታ ሃገር ፈጻምን ሓጋግን ፍርዳውን መሓውራት ብሒቱ፡ ግጉያት ፖሊሲታት ብምሕንጻጽን ግዕዘይ ፖለቲካ ብምትእትታውን ንኤርትራ "ኣብ ሞንጎ ናይ ምህላውን ምጥፋእን ሓደጋ" ኣሳጢሕዋ ከም ዘሎ እዩ ዘንጸባርቕ።

እንታይ ክግበር ኣልዎ? ንዝብል ሕቶ፡ ዶክተር በረኸት ለውጢ ኣብ ምምጻእ ሰለስተ ኣማራጺታት፡ -

ቀዳማይ፡ ነቲ ክንገብሮ ዝጸናሕና ከም ቀደሙ ክንቅጽሎ፡

ካልኣይ፡ ስዕረትና ኣሚና ብሕጊ ኣልቦ ስርዓት ኣሜን ኢልና ክንግዛእ፡

ሳልሳይ ድማ ካብቲ ኣብ ከይዲ ቃልሳዊ ጉዕዞ ክንክተሎ ዝጸናሕና ግጉይ ኣገባብ ወጺእና ካልእ ኣማራጺ ከነናዲ፡

ዝብላ ነጥብታት እዩ ኣልዒሉ።

እዛ ሳልሰይቲ ኣማራጺት፡ ከተዐውተና እትኽእል ኡንኮ ኣማራጺት ምዃና ኣሚኑ ድማ፡ ኣብ ሓድነት ዝተሞርከሰ ስሙር ግንባር ምምስራት ዝብል እማመ ኣቕሪቡ። እዚ ናይ ሓድነት ግንባር ግን፡ እቲ ናይ 'ቲ ስርዓት ምውዳቕ ዒላማ ምስተረጋገጸ፡ ዝኾነ ይኹን ሰብ ወይ 'ውን ጉጅለ ኣብቲ ስሙር ግንባር ናይ ምጽናሕ ግዴታ ከምዘይምልከቶ ብምስምማዕ ክምስረት ከም ዝግባእ ኣስሚሩሉ ኣሎ።

ከምቲ ዶክተር በረኸት ባዕሉ ዝሰማምዓሉ፡ እዚ ነገር ቅድሚ ሎሚ ተፈቲኑ ኣብ ግብሪ ንከይውዕል ዝዓንቀፉ ሓንኮልቲ ሓሳባት ምንባሮም ኣብ 'ዚ ጽሑፍ ከድህስሶ ፈቲኑ ኣሎ። ኣገባብ ቃልስና ሰላማዊ ዶ ጎነጻዊ? ምስ ኢትዮጵያ ዝህልወና ዝምድና ብቐረባ ዶ ብርሑቕ? ተራ ሲቪካውያን ማሕበራትን ፖለቲካውያን ሰልፍታትን እንታይ እዩ? ፍትሒ ዶ ሰላምን ዕርቅን ከነቐድም ይግባእ? ተራ ናይ ኣብ ወጻኢ ዝነብር ህዝብና ነቲ ኣብ ውሽጢ ኤርትራ ዘሎ ምንቅስቓስ ክሕግዝን ከተባብዕን ዶ ወይስ ነቲ ናይ ለወጢ ምንቅስቓስ ክመርሕ? እቲ ኣብ 1997 ዝጸደቐ ቅዋም ከም መሰረት ናይ ለውጢ ክንጥቀመሉ ኣሎና ዶ ወይስ ኣብ ቅዋማውነት ከነተኩር? ዝብሉ ሕቶታት ኣብ 'ዚ ጽሑፍ ኣነጺሩ ኣስፊርዎም ኣሎ። እንተኾነ ግን፡ ኣብ ወርቂ ሽሓኒ ዝተቐረበ ዝተወድአ መምርሒ ኣይኮነን ቀሪቡልና። ብኣንጻሩ ብዙሓት ዝተጠጅኡ ናይ ምርጫ ሓሳባት ኣብ ትሕቲ 'ቲ ኣገዳስነቱ ልዑል ምኻኑ ዝኣምነሉ ናይ ስሙር ግንባር ጥርናፈ፡ ከም ናይ መካትዒ ኣማራጺታት ቀሪቡልና ኣሎ። ዶክተር በረኸት፡ ከምቲ ለኒን ዝበሎ ነዚ ንኤርትራ ኣጋጢምዋ ዘሎ ወሳኒ ናይ ህላውነት ሕቶ ንክንገጥሞ መታን ክንዮ “ምውልዋልን ምፍንጫልን፡ ምፍራስን” ክንምርሽ ይግባኣና ኢሉ።

ቀዳማይ ቃል

==========❖==========

ሳሙኤል ቢዘን

ብመጀመርታ ነቲ ባሃር ኤርትራዊ ምሁር ናይ ዕድመ በዓል ጸጋ ኮይኑ ሃብታም ተሞኩሮኡ ከካፍለና ዘኽኣሎ ልዑል ፈጣሪ ከመስግን እፈቱ። ኤርትራ ከም ዶክተር በረኸትን ካልኦት መዛንኡ ዝወለደት ክነሳ ወላድ መኻን ኮይና ኣብዚ ዘላቶ ደረጃ ወዲቓ ምርኣይ ኣዝዩ ዘሕዝን ተርእዮ እዩ። እዚ ኮይኑ ግን፡ መሰል ብቃልሲ ዝረጋገጽ መስርሕ ስለዝኾነ፡ ዶክተር በረኸት ነቲ ናይ ልዕሊ 60 ዓመታት እኩብ ሞያዊ ዓቕሙን ናይ ቃልሲ ተሞክሮኡን ጾሚቑ ነዛ "ኣብ መስርሕ ቃልሳዊ ጉዕዞ ክንዓሞን ከነወግዶን ዝግባኣና ነገራት" እትብል ጽሕፍቲ ከበርክተልና ምኽኣሉ ከየመስገንክዎ ክሓልፍ ኣይደልን። ኣብዛ ጽሕፍቲ፡ ዶክተር በረኸት ነዚ ናይ ዓሰርተ ዓመታት ሓድሽ ናይ ቃልሲ ተመኩሮ ምስ ናይ ግዜ ገድሊ ተመክሮ ብምግንዛብን ብምንጽጻርን፡ ንምንታይን ብኸመይን ደረጃ፡ ደምበ-ተቓውሞ ኣብዚ ናይ ሕጂ ደረጃ ወዲቑ ይርከብ ምህላዉ ብዝርዝር ኣብሪህዎ ኣሎ። ኣብ ርእሲኡ፡ ነዚ ዘሎናዮ ኩነታት ንከንርዳእ፡ ከነልዕሎም ዘሎና ኣገደስቲ ሕቶታት ብምጥቃስ ናብ ፍታሕ ገጽና ንከነምርሕ ከነማልኦም ዝግብኣና ነገራትን ሓቢሩ ኣሎ።

ከም ርድኢተይ፡ ትሕዝቶ ናይ 'ዛ ጽሕፍቲ ነዚ ተፈናጪሉ ከድምዕ ዘይከኣለ ደምበ-ተቓውሞ ብሓፈሻ፡ ንዲሞክራስያውን ቅዋማውን ለውጢ ተባሂሉ ዝግበር ናይ ነፍሲ ወከፍ ዜጋ ጻዕርታት ድማ ብፍላይ፡ ጥሙር ቃልሲ ብምክያድ ነቲ ዝድለ ለውጢ ኣብ ምርግጋጽ ሓጋዚ ተራ ኣለዋ እብል። ኩሉ ንቅዋማዊ ለውጢ እቃለስ ኣለኹ ዝብል ኣካል፡ ብፍላይ ድማ እዚ ሓድሽ ወለዶ ንቀንዲ መልእኽቲ ናይዛ ጽሕፍቲ ብህድኣትን ብምስትውዓልን

ብምምርማርን ተመልኪቱ፡ ነቲ ዝጸንሐ ፋሕፋሕ ዝበለ ኣካይዳ በዲሁ፡ ቅልጡፍ ለውጢ ክረጋግጽ ይኽእል እዩ ዝብል ጽኑዕ እምነት ድማ ኣሎኒ። ንመልእኽቲ ናይ ‘ዚ ኣቦ "ኣብ መስርሕ ቃልሳዊ ጉዕዞ . . . " ኣንብብዋ። መጀመርታ ከም ተቓለስቲ ንዓኹም ክትልውጠኩም’ያ፡ ንስኹም ድማ ነቲ ናይ ሓባር ቃልሲ ክትልውጥዎ ኢኹም፡ ሽዑ ድማ እቲ ዝድለ ለውጢ ክረጋገጽ ግድን እዩ። እንተምንታይሲ፡ ቃልሲ ነብስኻ ብምልዋጥ ስለዝጅምር።

ንለውጢ እንዳሰራሕና ከሎና፡
ከነማልአምን ከነወግዶም ዝግብኣ ነገራት

==========❖==========

ብበረኸት ሃብተስላሴ
ፍሉይ ፕሮፌሰር ናይ ኣፍሪቃዊ ምርምርን
ናይ ሕጊ ፕሮፌሰርን ኣብ ዩኒቨርስቲ ሰሜን ካሮላይና ቻፕል ሂል

ኣብ ፕሪቶርያ ኣብ ናይ ኤርትራ ዓውደ መጽናዕቲ ዝቐረበ ጽሑፍ
ግንቦት 9 - 11 2014

ብመጀመርታ ቅርጺ ኣቀማምጣ ናይ'ዚ ሰነድ ንምሕባር፡

እዚ ጽሑፍ ኣብ ሓሙሽተ ኣርእስትታት ዝተኸፍለ እዩ። እቲ ቀዳማይ ክፋል መእተዊ፣ እቲ ካልኣይ ክፋል ነቲ ኣጋጢሙና ዘሎ ፖለቲካውን ቁጠባውን ማሕበራውን ቅልውላዋት፡ ትንተናን መብርህን ዝህብ፣ እቲ ሳልሳይ ክፋል ድማ ነቲ ልዕል ኢሉ ዝተገልጸ ጸገማት ንምፍታሕ ክውሰዱ ዘለዎም ስጉምትታት ዝሓቁፍ እዩ። እቲ ራብዓይ ክፋል፡ ንመጻኢ ዝጠመተ ኮይኑ ኣብ ግምት ከኣትዉ ኣለዎም ዝበልክዎም ኣገደስቲ ሕቶታት ኣልዒለ፡ ንኣይ ከም ውልቀ ዝረኣዩኒ መፍትሒታት ጠቒሰ ኣለኹ። ኣብ 'ቲ ሓሙሻይን ደምዳሚን ክፋል ናይ 'ዚ "ኣብ ከይዲ ቃልሳዊ ጉዕዞ" ዘርእስቱ ጽሑፈይ ድማ፡ ብታሪኻዊ ኣጠማምታ ኣከራኺርቲ ዝኾኑ ነጥብታት ኣልዒለ፡ ንኣታቶም ኣብ ምፍታሕ፡ ኣገዳስነት ቅዋም ማዕረ ክንደይ ዕዙዝ ምዃኑን ክጻወቶ ዝኽእል ተራን ክገልጽ እየ።

ኣብዚ እዋን እዚ ተቓዉሞታት ብዝተፈላለየ መልክዑ ኣንጻር እቲ ኣብ ኣስመራ ዘሎ ዲክታቶርያዊ ስርዓት እንዳዓበየ ይመጽእ ኣሎ። ነዚ ስርዓት ብናይ ሓባር ቃልሲ ንምእላዩ ከኣ ብዙሓት ግዱሳት ዜጋታት ዝተፈላለዩ ሓሳባትን ጻዊዒትን ኣቕሪቦም 'ዮም። ነዚ ጽሑፍ እዚ ከዳሉ ዝደረኸኒ ቀንዲ ረቛሒ ምኽንያት እምብኣር፡ ነቲ ኣብ ኣስመራ ዘሎ ስርዓት ንምእላይ ኣብ ዝግበር ናይ ሓባር ቃልሲ፡ ንክትዕን ምይይጥን ክጠቅም ዝኽእል ሓፈሻዊ መወከሲ ጽሑፍ ኣዳልየ፡ ኣብ ምስላጥ ናይ 'ቲ እነካይዶ ዘሎና ቃልሲ ሓጋዚ ተራ ክጻወት ይኽእል እዩ ካብ ዝብል እምንቶ ተበጊሰ እጃመይ ከበርክት ስለዝደለኹ እዩ።

መእተዊ

ኣብ ዘሎናዮ ናይ መሰጋገሪ እዋን፡ ነዚ ኣብ ሃገርና ተኸሲቱ ዘሎ ጸገማት ኣለሊና ነቲ ኣብ ድሕረ ናይ ኢሳያስ ስርዓት ክንተኽሎ ንእንደሊ ስርዓት ሓባሪ መንገዲ ክኾነና መታን፡ ንህሉው ኩነታትና ብዝተጸምቀ መንገዲ ከም ድሕረ ባይታ ከነቕምጦ ኣገዳስነት ኣለዎ። ብዙሓት ግዱሳት ተጣበቕትን፡ ምሁራት ዜጋታትን ነዚ ኣጋጢሙና ዘሎ ሽግር ብከመይ ክንገጥሞ ኣሎና ዝብሉ ሕቶታት ኣልዒሎም ብዙሕ ኣኼባታትን ምምይያጣታትን ኣካይዶም እዮም። ኣብ 'ዚ ቀረባ እዋናት ድማ፡ ንሃገራዊ ምርድዳእን ንናይ ስራሕ ምውህሃድን ዝጠልቡ ብዙሓት ጻዕርታት ክካየዱ ተዓዚብና ኣሎና። እዞም ኩሎም ጻዕርታት ዘርኣይዎ ናይ ሓሳባት ተመሳሳልነት ዝምስጥ እዩ። ነዚ ኩነታት ዝተዓዘበ ኩሉ ድማ፡ ምድግጋም ኣወጊዱ፡ ግዜን ንዋትን ዓቂቡ ብዝተዋሃሃደ ናይ ሓባር ስጉሚ ንቕድሚት ክምርሽ እዩ ዝምነ። ዕላማ ናይዛ ጽሕፍቲ እምበኣር፡ ሽቶና ንክንወቅዕ ሓድነት ናይ ስራሕ ኣብ ምርግጋጽ ክሕግዙና ዝኽእሉ ንጹራትን ዝተወሃሃዱን ሓሳባት ምብርካት እዩ። ኣብ 'ቶም ኣካታዕቲ ዝኾኑ ኣርእስትታት፡ እዛ ጽሕፍተይ ፍርዳዊት ንከይትኸውን፡ ነቲ ናይ ሶቅራጦስ ሓታቲ ኣገባብ ተኸቲለ ንክኸይድ እየ መሪጸ፡ ብዘይካ ኣብቶም ኣብ ቅዋም ረጊጽና ናይ ሓባር ረብሓ እነረጋግጸሎም ናይ ሃገር ህላወ መሰረት ዝኾኑ ኣርእስታት። ንጸገማትና መፍትሒታት ኣብ ምንዳይ ሓገዝቲ ንክኾኑ፡ ንገለ ገለ ኣካታዕቲ ዝኾኑ ኣርእስትታት ከም ኣብ እዋን ብረታዊ ቃልሲ ዝተፈጸሙ ገበናት ዝኣመሰሉ ጉዳያት ኮነ ኢለ ንኽትዕ ከፉታት ገዲፈዮም ኣለኹ።

ነዚ ዘሕዝን ክፋል ናይ ታሪኽና መፍትሒ ኣብ ምንዳይ፡ ገለ ሰባት ካብ ቅኑዕ መንፈስ ተበጊሶም ሽግራትና ብውልቀሰባት ብዝወሃብ ኣስተምህሮታት ዘይኮነ ዝፍታሕ፡ ኣብ መንጎ ኤርትራውያን ብዝግበር ዓሚቕ ዝርርብ እዩ ፍታሕ ክረክብ ዝኽእል ኢሎም ክሓስቡ ይኽእሉ 'ዮም። እንተኾነ ግን ከምዚ ዓይነት ኣስተምህሮ፡ ሃገራዊ ክትዕ ኣላዒሉ ኣብ ናይ ሓባር ምርድዳእ ንክንበጽሕ፡ እንታይ ክንገብር ይግባኣና ኣብ ዝብል ሃገራዊ ምይይጥ ክመርሓና ሓጋዚ ኣበርክቶ ኣለዎ ኢለ እኣምን። ንኣብነት፡ እቲ ኣብ 'ዚ ቀረባ እዋን ብኽቡር ሓው

ተወልደ ተስፋማርያም (ወዲ ቫካሮ) ዝተገብረ ህዝባዊ ኣስተምህሮ ዘብርሃልና ጉዳይ እንተ ሃልዩ፡ ካብ ልቢ ዝነቐለን ብስምዒት ዝተደረኸን ምስ ዝኸውን፡ ኣብ ዝበዝሐ ክፋል ሕብረተ ሰብ ኤርትራ ጽልዋ ከምዝህልዎ ርዱእ እዩ። ድሕሪ ናይ ወዲ ቫካሮ ህዝባዊ ኣኼባታት፡ ገለ ሰባት ካብዚ ከ ናበይ? እዚ ምንቅስቓስ ናበየናይ ዝተጨበጠ ተግባራት ክመርሓና እዩ? ዝበሉ ሕቶታት ኣቕሪቦም እዮም። እዞም ሕቶታት ኣገደስቲ ኮይኖም ንኣይ 'ውን ናብ 'ዚ ኣብዛ ጽሕፍቲ ክምልሶ ተቐሪበ ዘለኹ ቀንዲ ሕቶታት እዮም መሪሖምኒ። ንሱ ድማ እቲ ዝድለ ለውጢ ንምርግጋጽ እንታይ ዓይነት ዝተጨበጠ ስጉምቲ ክውሰድ ኣለዎ ዝብል እዩ።

እዚ ኣብ ፕሪቶርያ ዝተዳለወ ዓውደ-መጽናዕቲ ንገለ ካብቶም ኣብ ኤርትራ ተፈጢሮም ዘለዉ ሽግራት ዘርዚርዎም ኣሎ። ንኣቀራርባ ክጥዕም መታን፡ ፖለቲካውን ቁጠባውን ማሕበራውን ኣብ ዝብሉ ኣርእስትታት ከፋፊለ ከቕርቦም እየ። ብኡ መሰረት ድማ ነዞም መሰረት ሽግራትና ዝኾኑ ኣገደስቲ ነጥብታት ምስ ታሪኻዊ ኩነታትና ኣገናዚበ ክገልጾም 'የ።። ንኤርትራ ዝምልከቱ ጉዳያት፡ ብፍላይ ድማ ምስ ታሪኽ ብረታዊ ቃልስና ዝተኣሳሰር ክልተ ዝተፈላለየ ኣዘናታትዋ ኣሎ። እዚ ኣዘናታትዋ ምስቲ ዝነበረ ታሪኻዊ ኣጠማምታ ናይ ክልተ ውዱባት [ተጋድሎ ሓርነት ኤርትራ (ጀብሃ) ን ናይ ህዝባዊ ግንባር ሓርነት ኤርትራ (ሻዕብያ)ን] ነቲ ኣብ መንጎኦም ዝነበረ ናይ ውድድር መንፈስ ዘንጸባርቕ ፍልልያት እዩ ነይሩ። ኣብዚ ቀረባ እዋን ግን፡ እቲ ናይ ውድድር መንፈስ እናረሓቐ ናብ ክተዓረቑሉ ዝኽእሉ ኩነታት ኣምሪሖ ንዕዘብ ኣሎና። ኣብ 'ዚ ኣብ ሓደ ዕላማ ረጊጽና ንናይ ሓባር ጸላኢ ንክንገጥም ንሸባሸበሉ ዘለና እዋን ምኽሳቱ ድማ ኣዝዩ ዘተባብዕ እዩ።

እቲ ዝበረኸ ጸገማትን ኣገደስቲ ረቛሒታትን

ኤርትራ ድሕሪ ናይ ልዕሊ ዕስራ ዓመታት ነጻነት ኣብ ፈታኒ ናይ ታሪኽ መድረኽ ኣትያ ህላውነታ ኣብ ሓደጋ ወዲቑ ክንርኢ ንቡር ኮይኑ ጸኒሑ ኣሎ። እቲ ኣብ ላምፐዱሳ ዘጋጠመ ህልቂት ኤርትራውያን፡ ነቲ ዘጓነፈ መሪር ናይ ታሪኽ ኣጋጣሚ ቋሕ ኢልና ክንጥምቶን ነቲ መሪር ሓዘን ተገዲድና ክንውሕጦን ጌሩና 'ዩ። እዚ ተጋሂዱ ዘሎ ሓቂ እምበኣር እቶም ዋሕስ ናይ መጻኢ ትውልዲ ዝኾኑ መንእሰያት ተስፋ-ኣልቦ ኮይኖም መጻኢኦም ኣብ ዘየማዕድዉሉ ኩነታት ሸሚምዎም ይርከብ ኣሎ። ብዘይ ትስፉው መንእሰይ ድማ፡ ሓንቲ ሃገር ብሩህ መጻኢ ኣይህልዋን። እቲ ኣዝዩ ዘሕዝን ጉዳይ ድማ እቲ ዲሞክራስን ምዕባለን ልዕልና ሕግን ከረጋግጽ ቃል ዝኣተወ መንግስቲ ኤርትራ፡ ቀንዲ ጠንቂ ናይ 'ዚ መወዳእታ ዘይብሉ ግጭታትን፡ ስቓይን ተስፋ ሙቕራጽን ኮይኑ ምህላዉ እዩ። መንግስቲ ኢሳይያስ ኣፍወርቅን እቲ ንሱ

ዝመርሖ ሰልፊ ህዝባዊ ግንባር ንደሞክራስን ፍትሕን (ህግደፍ) ንህዝቢ ኤርትራ ዲሞክራሲ ይኹን ፍትሒ ኣየምጽኣሉን። ብኣንጻሩ ንዝኣተውዎ መብጽዓ ጠሊሞም፡ ነቲ ዉሑድ ኣታዊ ሃገር ኣባኺኖም፡ ንዝነበሮም ወርቃዊ ዕድል ተሓሲሞም፡ ሓደገኛ ፖለቲካን ኣዕናዊ ፖሊሲታትን ብምትእትታው ረብሓ ሃገር ኣባኺኖም። በቲ ብስም “ሃገራዊ ኣገልግሎት” ዝጽዋዕ ግዱድ ወፍሪ ዕስክርናን ስራሕን ኣቢሎም ድማ ንመንእሰያት ኤርትራ ወርቃዊ ኣፍራዪ ዕድሚኦም ኣባኺኖም ኣብ መወዳእታ ዘይብሉ ዕስክርና ቆሪኖም፡ ዕድሚኦም ምሉእ ኣብ በረኻ ከርተት ክብሉን ንዝሸምገሉ ወለዶም ንከይጥውሩ ዕድል ተነፊግዎም ኣይትምህርቲ ኣይሓዳር ኮይኖም ይርከቡ ኣለዉ። ካብዚ ደረት-ኣልቦ ባርነት ድሕሪ ምህዳሞም እዮም ድማ እዞም መንእሰያት ኣብ ላምፐዱሳ ዝጠሓሉ። ካልኦት ውሑድ ቁጽሪ ዘለዎም መንእሰያት’ውን፡ ቅድሚ’ዚ ናይ ላምፐዱሳ ሓደጋ ኣብ ማእከላይ ባሕሪ ምጥሓሎም ዝዝከር ‘ዩ።

እስከ ነቶም ብሰሪ ናይ ላምፐዱሳ ህልቂት ኣጋጣሚ ዝተጋህዱ ዘሕዝኑ ጸገማት ብሕጽር ዝበለ ክንርእዮም ክንፍትን፡

- ንሕግን ቅጥዕን ዓለማዊ ኣካይዳ ይኹን ነቲ ኣብ 1997 ዝጸደቐ ቅዋምና ብምጥሓስ ቀጻሊ ግህሰት መሰረታዊ ሰብኣዊ መሰላት ይፍጸም ኣሎ።
- እዛ ሃገር ብመምርሒታት ፈጻሚ ቤት-ጽሕፈት ናይ ብህዝቢ ዘይተመርጸ ፕረሲደንት ትማሓደር ኣላ። እዚ መምሪሒታት ‘ዚ ድማ ዝኾነ ዓይነት ምምማይ ዘይግበረሉን ብተግባር ድማ ንልዕልና ሕጊ ዝጥሕስን እዩ።.
- እቲ ኣብ ኮረሻ ስልጣን ተኾይጡ ዝመርሕ ዘሎ ናይ ህ.ግ.ደ.ፍ. ሰልፊ ንብሙሉኡ ቁጠባ ናይቲ ሃገር ብመንገዲ ‘ቲ ብስም ቀይሕ ባሕሪ ዝፍለጥ መጋበርያኡ ዝኾነ ትካልን ካልኦት ንኡሳን ጨናፍራቱን ጌሩ ኣብ ትሕቲ ሙሉእ ምቁጽጻሩ ኣእትይዎ ይርከብ።
- እቲ ስርዓት ኣብ ወተሃደራዊ ዕንደራ ጥሒሉ ነቲ ሕብረተ ሰብ ኣብ መወዳእታ ዘይብሉ “ወተሃደራዊ ኣገልግሎት” ቆሪንዎ ይርከብ። ኩሉ ኤርትራዊ ኣብ ክሊ ዕድመ ናይ 18ን 50ን ዝርከብ ከምኡ ‘ውን ኣብ መንጎ 18ን 40ን ክሊ ዕድመ ዝርከባ ደቂ ኣንስትዮ ንዘይተወሰነ ግዜ ብረት ከዓጥቁ ይግደዱ ኣለዉ።
- ከም ውጽኢት ናይ ‘ዚ ኩነታት ድማ መላእ ሕብረተሰብ ኤርትራ ማሕበራውን ቁጠባውን ምፍንቓላትን፡ ናይ ትምህርትን ሞያውን ዕድላት ምምዝባላትን ኣጓኒፍዎ ይርከብ ኣሎ።

- ብዓቢኡ ድማ፡ እቲ ናብ ዲሞክራስያዊትን ብቅዋም እትመሓደር ሃገር ናይ ምህናጽ መብጽዓ ተጠሊሙ፡ ሃገርና ኣብ ትሕቲ ብሓደ ሰልፊ ዝምራሕ ጨፍላቒ ስርዓት ተቖሪና ትርከብ ኣላ። እዚ ክስተት 'ዚ ድማ ነቲ ኣብ ክልተ ጉባኤታት ናይ 'ቲ ሰልፊ ዝሓለፈ ውሳኔታት ይኹን ናይ 'ቲ ኣብ 1997 ዝጸደቐ ቅዋም ዓንቀጻት ብምጥሓስ ዝተወስደ ኮይኑ፡ ንሃገርና ኣብ ዓሚቕ ቅልውላው ሸሚምዋ ይርከብ ኣሎ።

መሰረታውያን ጠንቅታት ቅልውላው

ናይ ምግባትን ምንጻልን ፖለቲካ

ከምቲ ኣብ ላዕሊ ተገሊጹ ዘሎ፡ እቲ መንግስቲ ብፕረሲደንት ኢሳይያስ ኣፍወርቂ ብዝምራሕ ናይ ሓደ ሰልፊ ናይ ስልጣን ዓብላልነት ዝተባሕተ እዩ። ዋላኳ ስማዊ ዝኾነ ምክፍፋል ስልጣን ኣብቶም ሰለስተ ኣካላት መንግስቲ ማለት ሓጋጊን ፈጻሚን ፈራዲን ኣካላት እንተሃለወ፡ እቲ ብኢሳይያስ ዝምራሕ ፈጻሚ ኣካል ንኹሉ ስራሓት መንግስቲ ኣብ ትሕቲ ምሉእ ምቁጽጻሩ ብምእታው፡ ኣብ ልዕሊ ልዕልና ሕግን ምክፍፋል ስልጣን ከሸካዕልል ይርከብ ኣሎ።

ኩሉ ነገር ኣብ ትሕቲ ሓደ ሰብን ውሑዳት ዝምእዘዝዎ ኣባላት እቲ ሰልፍን ተማእኪሉ ይርከብ። እቶም ዞባውያን ምምሕዳራት እንተኾኑ 'ውን መቖጻጸልታ ናይ 'ቲ ማእከላዊ ስልጣን ኮይኖም፡ ኣብ 'ተን ሽዱሽተ ዞባውያን ምምሕዳራት ዝተመዘዙ ኣማሓደርቲ በቲ ፕረሲደንት ዝተመርጹ 'ዮም። ካብ 2002 ኣትሒዙ ድማ እዘን ምምሕዳር ዞባታት ብመሰረት ፕረሲደንታዊ ድንጋጌ ጸብጻባተን ናብ 'ቶም ናይ 'ተን ዞባታት ወተሃደራዊ ሓለፍቲ ጀነራላት ከም ዘቕርባ ተጌሩ። እቶም ጀነራላት ድማ ብግዲኦም ጸብጻቦም ናብ ፕረሲደንት የመሓላልፉ። እዚ ኩነታት ነቲ መንግስቲ ናብ ፍጹም ወተሃደራዊ ምሕደራ ቀይሩ፡ ነቲ ሕብረተ-ሰብ ይኹን ነቲ ሲቪላዊ ኣመራርሓ ናይ ህዝቢ ኣብ ራዕዲ ተዋሒጡ ሓገዝ ኣልቦ ኮይኑ ከምዝተርፍ ጌርዎ።

ሓደ ካብቶም ዓበይቲ መግለጺታት ናይ 'ቲ ኣብ ኤርትራ ኣጋጢሙ ዘሎ ዓበይቲ ፖለቲካዊ ጸገማት፡ ኣብ 'ቲ ሃገር ተሓታትነትን ግሉጽነት ዘይምህላዉ እዩ። እዚ ስለዝኾነ እዩ ድማ፡ እቲ ሓላፍነት ዘይስምዖ ፕረሲደንት ንካቢነ ሚኒስተራትን ሃገራዊ ባይቶን ከየማኸረ ኣብ 1998 ብውልቁ ምስ ኢትዮጵያ ኲናት ኣዊጁ። ድሕሪ እቲ ኣዕናዊ ኲናት ላዕለዎት ሰበስልጣን መንግስትን ውድብን ነቲ ፕረሲደንት ዝወሰዶ በይናዊ ስጉምቲ ብምቅዋም ነቲ ሃገር ናብ ኲናት ንክትኣቱ ዝገበረ ውሳነን፡ ነቲ ናይ ኢትዮጵያ ሰራዊት ሰፊሕ ክፋል

መሬት ኤርትራ ክሕዝ ዘኽኣሎ ጠንቂ ምኽንያት ክምርምሩ ኣኼባ ክካየድ ጠሊቦም። ብኣጠቓላሊ እቶም ካብ ግዜ ሓርነታዊ ቃልሲ ኣትሒዞም ብጾቱ ዝነበሩ፡ ኣብቲ ንዓመታት ብሒትዎ ዝጸንሐ መንግስቲ መሳርሕቱ ዝነበሩ፡ ሕጂ ብጉጅለ-15 ዝጽውዑ ሰባት ንመጀመርታ ግዜ ንኢሳይያስ ክብድህዎ ጀሚሮም። ከም ኣባላት ካቢነ ሚኒስተራትን ላዕለዎት ሓለፍቲ ናይ 'ቲ ውድብን ንዓኣቶምን ንሃገራዊ ባይቶን ከይሓተተ ነቲ ኲናት ብምጅማሩ ክሕተት ከምዝግብኦ ጠለቦም ኣቕሪቦም። እቲ ናይ ፕረሲደንት ግብረ-መልሲ ግን ትዕቢት ዝመልኦ ምንጻግን ምፍርራሕ ዝተሓወሶን፡ ጠለባቶም እንተ ዘይኣቋሪጾም 'ውን ኣብ ልዕሊኦም ሕማቕ ሳዕቤን ከኸትል ምዃኑን ዝሕብር እዩ ኔሩ።

ኣብ ጽባሕ 11 መስከረም 2001፡ ዓለም ናብ 'ቲ ኣብ ኣሜሪካ ዘጋጠመ ግብረ-ሽበራዊ መጥቃዕቲ ኣድሂባ ኣብ ዝነበረትሉ እዋን፡ ኢሳይያስ ን12 ኣባላት ጉጅለ-15 ኣብ ቀይዲ ንኽኣትዉ ኣዚዙ። ኣብ ርእሲኡ 'ውን፡ ነቶም ናይተን ኣብ 'ቲ እዋን ዕሸላት ዝነበራ ናይ ብሕቲ ጋዜጣታት ሓለፍትን ጸሓፍትን ዝኾኑ ጋዜጠኛታት፡ ነቲ ካብ ህዝቢ ይኹን ካብ ኣባላት ጉጅለ 15 ናብ መንግስቲ ዝቐርብ ዝነበረ ነቐፌታዊ ጽሑፋት ይኹን፡ ነቲ ምስ ኣባላት ጉጅለ-15 ዝግበር ዝነበረ ቃለ-ምልልስ ኣኣንጊድኩም ተባሂሎም ኣብ ትሕቲ ሞቑሕ ናይ 'ቲ ስርዓት ከም ዝኣትዉ ተገብረ። እዚ ምእሳር ናይዞም 12 ኣባላት ጉጅለ-15ን ጋዜጠኛታትን ነቲ ኣብ ወጻኢ ሃገር ዝርከብ ህዝቢ ከነቓቕሕን ሕቶታት ኣልዒሎም ኣንጻር እቲ ስርዓት ተቓውሞታቶም ከጎሃህሩን ደሪኹ 'ዩ። ብመንግስቲ ንዝተፈጸሙ ምግሃስ ሰብኣዊ መሰላት ንክጻረን ንትግባረ ናይቲ ኣብ 1997 ዝጸደቐ ቅዋም ዝጠልባ ሓደሽቲ ፖለቲካውያን ሰልፍታትን ሲቪካውያን ማሕበራት ክዕንብባ ጀሚረን።

ናይ ኢሳይያስ ግብረ-መልሲ ግን ኣንጻር ናይ 'ቲ ብጉጅለ-15 ዝቐረበ ሕቶታትን ኣንጻር ትጽቢታትን ተስፋን ናይ 'ቶም ብሃገሮም ዝግደሱን ዝሓልዩን መስተውዓልቲ ክፋል ሕብረተ-ሰብ ኤርትራ ዝቐንዐ እዩ ኔሩ። ፕረሲደንት ኢሳይያስ ናይ ሃገራዊ ባይቶ ኣኼባ ኣካይዱ 'ዩ፡ እንተኾነ ግን እቲ ኣኼባ ነቲ ናይ ጉጅለ -15 ጠለባት ንምምላእ ዘይኮነ፡ ብኣንጻሩ ንጉጅለ-15 ብጥልመት ሃገርን ካልኦት ገበናትን ዝውንጅል እማመ ንምቕራብ እዩ ኔሩ። እቲ ዳርጋ ሙሉእ ብሙሉእ ዝተቐጻጸሮ ሃገራዊ ባይቶ ድማ ከምቲ ዝተባህሎ ነቲ ዝቐረበ እማመ ናይ ክሲ ኣጽዲቕዎ። እቶም ኣብ 18 መስከረም 2001 ኣብ ትሕቲ ቀይዲ ዝኣተዉ 12 ኣባላት ናይ ጉጅለ-15 ድማ ክሳብ ሕጂ ሃለዋት ዘይብሎም ኣብ ዘይተፈልጠ ቤትማእሰርቲ ተሰዊሮም ይርከቡ። (እቶም ኣብ ወጻኢ ብምጽንሖም ካብ ማእሰርቲ ዘምለጡ ኣባላት ናይ 'ቲ ጉጅለ ድማ ኣብ 'ቲ ናይ ተቓውሞ ደምበ ተጸንቢሮም ይርከቡ።)

ብጻውዒት ፕረሲደንት ዝዝወር፡ ምእዙዝ ሃገራዊ ባይቶ ከምዘለና ተዓዚብና ኣሎና። እቲ ፍርዳዊ ኣካል ከ ዝብል ሕቶ ክለዓል ድማ ንቡር እዩ። ኣብ 1997 ናጽነት ፍርዳዊ ኣካል ዘውሕስ ቅዋም ብምጽዳቑ ክተኣታቶ ጀሚሩ ዝነበረ ትካላዊ ኣሰራርሓ ተስፋ ዝህብ እዩ ኔሩ። ፕረሲደንት ላዕለዋይ ቤት -ፍርዲ ንነጻነት ቤት ፍርዲ ንምውሓስን ህይወት ንምሃብን እቲ ፍርዳዊ ኣካል ካብ ምትእትታው ናይ ፈጻሚ ኣካል ነጻ ኮይኑንክሰርሕ ዝከኣሎ ጻዕሪ ኣካይዱ። ኣብ ኣስመራ ኣብ ዝተጋብአ ዓለምለኻዊ ዓውደ- መጽናዕቲ፡ ብዛዕባ ምትእትታው ፈጻሚ ኣካል ኣብ ፍርዳዊ ኣካል፡ ብፍላይ ድማ ምትእትታው ፕረሲደንት ናይ 'ቲ ሃገር ኣብ ፍርዳዊ መስርሕ ብቑሉዕ ነቒፉ።

ንምጥቃስ ዝኣክል፡ ነቲ ብፕረሲደንት ላዕለዋይ ቤትፍርዲ ዝቐረበ ነቐፌታዊ ሓሳባት ካብ ተሳተፍቲ ናይ 'ቲ ዓውደ-መጽናዕቲ ዋላ ሓደ ሰብ ድጋፍ ይኹን ሕቶ ወይ 'ውን ርእይቶ ዝሃበ ኣይነበረን። እቲ ነታ ሃገር ውሒጥዋ ዘሎ ስቕታ ኣብቶም ኤርትራውያን ጥራሕ ዝተደረተ ኣይነበረን፡ ዋላ እቶም ኣብቲ ዓውደ-መጽናዕቲ ክሳተፉ ዝመጹ ወጻእተኛታት ፈተውቲ ኤርትራ ከይተረፉ እዮም ተጸልዮም። ድሕሪ ቁሩብ መዓልታት ፕረሲደንት ኢሳያስ ነቲ ላዕለዋይ ዳኛ ናይ 'ቲ ሃገር፡ ካብ ስርሑ ንክእለ ኣዚዙ። ከም መራሒ መንግስቲን ዝለዓለ ሓላፊ ሓይልታት ምክልኻልን ምስኡ ዝተሓሓዘ ጸጥታዊ ኣገልግሎታትን ኮይኑ ነታ ሃገር ኣብ ትሕቲ ፍጹም ምቁጽጻር ኣእትይዋ ይርከብ። ብሓጺሩ እቲ ኣብ ናይ ውትህድርና መነባብሮ ተሸሚሙ ዘሎ ህዝቢ ምሉእ ብምሉእ ኣብ ትሓቲ 'ቲ ቃሉ ሕጊ ዝኾነ ዲክታተር ተረጊጹ ይነብር ኣሎ።

ምግባትን ምንፋግን ቁጠባ ሃገር

ኣብዚ እዋን እዚ ናይ ኤርትራ ቁጠባ ኣብ ዝተሓተ ደረጅኡ ወዲቑ ይርከብ። እቲ ርእሰ-ምርኮሳ ዝብል ጭርሓ፡ ዋላኳ ኣብ ግዜ ብረታዊ ቃልሲ ጠቓምነቱ ዕዙዝ ይንበር፡ ኣብዚ ዘሎናዮ እዋን ግዚኡ ኣእኪሉ ካብ ጥቕሚ ወጻኢ ኮይኑ ንቁጠባዊ ምዕባለ ሃገርና ንቕድሚት ንከይስጉም ሓሊኹ ሒዝዎ ይርከብ ኣሎ። ኣብ ርእሲ 'ዚ እቲ ካብ መንግስቲ ኢትዮጵያ ካብ ደርግ ዝተወርሰ ናይ "ምእኩል ቁጠባ" መምርሒ እንተኾነ 'ውን በቶም ማርክሰ ለኒንነት ንምምላስ ዝጣበቑ ናይ ህግደፍ ክልስ ሓሳባውያን መራሕቲ ክስራሓሉ ክንዕዘብ ጸኒሕና። ብሕታውያን ትካላት እቲ ካብ "ሕውስዋስ ቁጠባ" ዝብል መምርሒ ንክረኽብኦ ዝተኣትወለን መብጽዓ ተነፊግወን ኣሎ። እቲ ንኤርትራ ናብ ሲንጋፖር ክንቅይራ ኢና ዝብል ዝነበረ ናይ ህግደፍ መርሓ ናብ ፍጹም ውድቀት እዩ ኣምሪሑ። ብመጀመርትኡ፡ እቲ ንሲንጋፖር ናብ ቀዳማይ ደረጃ ቁጠባ ምዕባለ ክትሕንበብ ዝገበረ ረቛሒታት ኣብ ኤርትራ የለን። ናይ ኤርትራ ቁጠባ ኣብ ሕርሻ፡ ምርባሕ ከብትን ፈኪስ ኢንዳስትርን ዝተሓጽረ ብምኳኑ ንቅልጡፍ ቁጠባዊ ምዕባለ

መሰረት ዝኸውን ዓቕሚ የብሉን። እቶም ኣብ ሃብቲ ባሕርን ባህርያዊ ማዕድናትን ቱሪዝምን ንወፍሪ ክስሕቡ ዝኽእሉ ዝነበሩ ናይ ቁጠባ ጽላታት ‘ውን እንኳን ዶ ወፍሪ ክስሕቡ ብሰንኪ እቶም ግጉያት ፖሊሲታትን ዝንቡዕ ፖለቲካዊ መስመርን ኣብ ከውሒ ተጋጭዮም ተሓምሺሾም ተሪፎም።

መንግስቲ ኤርትራ ንናይ ሲንጋፖር ቅዲ ብምኽታል ንምምዕባል ዓቕሚ ሰብ ቀዳምነት ሂቡ ኣብ ኤርትራ ቁጠባዊ ሓርነት ከረጋግጽ ቃል ኣትዩ ነይሩ። ነዚ ንምዕዋት ‘ውን ምምሕዳራዊ ምምሕያሻት ከምጽእ ዘኽእል ፖሊሲታት ሓንጺጹ። እንተኾነ ግን እቲ ወተሃደራዊ ዕንደራ ንባጀት ናይ ‘ቲ ስርዓት ገቢቱ፡ እታ ሃገር ኣብ ትምህርትን ካልኦት ናይ ህዝቢ ኣገልግሎታት ተዳኺማ እቲ ናይ ኤርትራ ናይ ዓቕሚ ሰብ ምሕያል መደብ ተሰናኺሉ ተሪፉ። ብተወሳኺ፡ ንትምህርታዊ ፖሊሲ ብፍላይ ድማ ንናይ ላዕለዋይ ደረጃ ትምህርቲ ዝምልከት ህዝባዊ ክትዓትን ምይይጣት ኣይተኻየደን። እታ እንኮ ናይ ላዕለዋይ ደረጃ ትምህርቲ እተኣንግድ ዝነበረት ናይ ኣስመራ ዩኒቨርሲቲ በብቑሩብ ከምትዳኸምን ኣብ መወዳእታ ድማ ከም ትዕጾን ድሕሪ ምግባር ብኣብ ውሑዳት ቦታታት ዝተኸፍታ ብወተሃደራዊ ሓለፍቲ ዝምሓደራ ናይ ቴክኒክ ኮለጃት ከም ትትካእ ተጌሩ። ተማሃሮ ናይ’ዘን ካብ ውትህድርናን ትምህርትን ዝተሓናፈጻ ኮለጃት ካብ ግዱድ “ሃገራዊ ኣገልግሎት” ዝተሳሕቡ ኮይኖም ኣብ ዝኾነ እዋን ናብ ሰራዊት ክጽውዑ ዝኽእሉ እዮም። እቲ መንግስቲ ነዚ ከም ሓደ ብነጻ ጉልበት ተጠቒሙ ናብ ናይ ዕብየት መንገዲ ዝመርሕ ፕሮጀክት ጌሩ እዩ ክር እዮ ዝፍትን። እቲ ኣብ ባይታ ዝረአ ዘሎ ውጽኢት ግን ንዕኡ ዘንጸባርቕ ኣይኮነን። እዚ ፕሮጀክት ‘ዚ እቲ ዝድለ ውጽኢት ኣየምጽአን፡ ብኣንጻሩ ከም ‘ቲ ኣቐዲሙ ዝተጠቕሰ ምብኳን ሰብኣዊ ዓቕምን፡ ናይ ህዝቢ ስቅያትን ምብትታን ሕብረተ-ሰብን ጥራሕ እዩ ኣኸቲሉ።

ብኣጠቓላሊ፡ ኣብዘን ናይ ቀረባ ዓመታት ገምጋም ተሞርኪስና እቲ ቁጠባዊ ዕብየት ዋላኳ ምሉእ ብሙሉእ ኣንቀልቂሉ እንተዘይ ተባህለ ኣብ ሕማቕ ኩነታት እዩ ዝርከብ። ዋላ ‘ኳ ዕደናዊ ኣታዊታት ይሃሉ፡ እቲ ዓመታዊ ዕብየት ቁጠባ ሃገር ካብ 2 ሚእታዊት ንታሕቲ ክቕጽል   ኣብ ወጻኢ ሃገራት ካብ ዝርከቡ ኤርትራውያን ዝሰደድ ናይ ወጻኢ ሸርፊን እዩ። ብተወሳኺ እቲ መንግስቲ ንኣብ ወጻኢ ሃገር ዝርከቡ ኤርትራውያን ዜጋታት ነቲ ኣብ ውሽጢ ሃገር ክረኽብዎ ዝግባእ ማሕበራውን ሰብኣውን ኣገልግሎታት ከም መርዓ፡ ቀብሪን ካልእ ምስኡ ዝተሓሓዘ ዝተፈላለዩ ኣገልግሎታት ክረኽቡ እንተኾይኖም 2 ሚእታዊት ካብ ኣታዊኦም ክኸፍሉ የገድዶም ኣሎ። እዚ ኩሉ ምንፋግ ቁጠባዊ ናጽነት፡ ኣብ መነባብሮ ህዝብና ዘለዎ ጽልዋ ኣዝዩ ዓቢ ምዃኑ ንጹር እዩ።

ማሕበራዊ ምምሽማሽን መዐቀኒኡን

ናይ 'ታ ሃገር ማሕበራውን ቁጠባውን ፖሊቲካውን መዳያት ካብ ግዜ ናብ ግዜ እንዳኸፍአ ይመጽእ ኣሎ። ናይ ኤርትራ ኩነታት ንልዕሊ ዓሰርተ ዓመታት ብፍላይ ድማ ድሕሪ 'ቲ ካብ 1998 ክሳብ 2000 ምስ ኢትዮጵያ ዝተኻየደ መሪር ኲናት እንዳኸፍአ ክኸይድ ጸኒሑ። ዋላ ቅድሚ'ቲ ኣዕናዊ ኲናት እንተኾነውን፡ እቲ ዓብላልን ነጻልን ፖሊሲን ፖለቲካን ህግደፍ፡ ንኩሉ ምንቅስቓሳት ናይ 'ታ ሃገር ብሒቱ ካልኦት ናይ ፖለቲካ ሰልፍታት ኣብ ፖለቲካ ናይ 'ቲ ሃገር ንከይሳተፉ ዓንቂጹ፡ ንኹሉ ቁጠባዊ ንጥፈታት ናይ 'ታ ሃገር ዓብሊሉ ኣብ ትሕቲ ሙሉእ ምቁጽጻሩ እዩ ኣእትይዎ። ብመሰረት "ናይ ውዱብ ሕቡራት ሃገራት ሰብኣዊ ምዕባለ መዐቀኒ" (HDI), ኤርትራ ሓንቲ ካብተን ኣብ ዝተሓተ ደረጃ ዝሰርዓ ሃገራት እያ። ንኣብነት ኣብ 'ቲ ኣብ 2004 ዝተገብረ መዐቀኒ፡ 0.45 ነጥቢ ብምምዝጋብ ኣብ ዳርጋ መጨረሽታ፡ ካብ 177 መበል 157 ደረጃ ምሓዛ ዝዝከር እዩ። (ናይ ዩ.ኤን.ዲ.ፒ. ኤች.ዲ.ኣይ. ናይ 2006 ረፖርት ተመልከት)

ንኣብነት፡ ኤርትራ ብናይ ውዱብ ሕቡራት ሃገራት ናይ ምዕባለ ፕሮግራም (UNDP) ዓመታዊ ዝካየድ ናይ ሰብኣዊ ምዕባለ መዐቀኒ መሰረት መበል 182 ደረጃ ምሓዛ ካፒታል ኤርትራ ዝተባህለ ናይ ዜና ኣገልገሎት ገሊጹ። እዚ ብናይ ውዱብ ሕቡራት ሃገራት ናይ ምዕባለ ፕሮግራም ዝግበር መጽናዕቲ 187 ሃገራት ዘሳትፍ ኮይኑ፡ እዚ ናይ ሰብኣዊ ምዕባለ መዐቀኒ ነቲ ኣብታ ሃገር ዘሎ ማዕርነት፡ ትምህርቲ፡ ንውሓት ዕድመን ኣታውን ኣብ ግምት ብምእታው ከምዝካየድ እዩ እቲ ጸብጻብ ኣፍሊጡ። በዚ መዐቀኒታት መሰረት እያ እምበኣር ኤርትራ ንሓሙሽተ ሃገራት ብምቕዳም መበል 182 ደረጃ ሒዛ ዘላ። እቲ ጸብጻብ ነቲ ኣብ ዝሓለፈ ዓመት ኣብ ላምፐዱሳ ዘጋጠመ ናይ 300 ኤርትራውያን ህልቂት ኣብ ግምት ምእታዉ ይፍለጥ። (See UNDP HDI Report, 2006).

"መዐቀኒ ሰብኣዊ ምዕባለ" ሓደ ካብቶም ንኩሉ መዳያዊ ሰብኣዊ ኩነታት ንምዕቃን ክንዮ ናይ ውሽጣዊ ምዕባለ መዐቀኒ (ጂዲፒ) ዝኸይድ ኣገዳሲ መሳሪሒ እዩ። ንዝተፈላለዩ ኩርናዓት ሰብኣዊ ምዕባለ ኣብ ግምት ዘእቱ ኣብ ርእሲ ምዃኑ፡ ብቐንዱ ድማ ነቶም ኣገደስቲ ነገራት ከም ቀረብ ናይ ብቑዕ ዓቕንን መኣዛን ዘለዎ መግቢ፡ ኩሉ ብቐሊሉ ክረኽቦ ዝኽእል ትምህርቲ፡ እኹል ጥዕናዊ ኣገልግሎት፡ ኣብ ውሑስ ዝኾነ ከባቢ መንበሪ ብሕሱር ናይ ምርካብ ምዕባለታት የጠቓልል። ኣብ 2006 ዝተገብረ መጽናዕቲ ከም ዝሕብሮ ኤርትራ ንዝበዝሐ ክፋል ህዝባ ነዞም ኣብ ላዕሊ ዝተጠቕሱ ኣገልግሎታት ብዘይምቕራባ፡ ኣብ ኣዝያ ትሑት ሰብኣዊ ምዕባለ ከምእትርከብ ሕቶ ዘድልዮ ኣይኮነን።

ኩሩዕን ጻዕራምን ህዝቢ ናብ ደረጃ ናይ ምልማን ወሪዱ፡ ካብ ለገስቲ ሃገራት ካብ ዝርከብ መሰረታዊ ናይ መግቢ ረዲኤት ተመጽዋቲ ክኸውን ተገዲዱ። ዋላኳ ካብ ቀደም ኣትሒዙ፡ ነቲ ሽግር ኣብ ምግዳድ ድርቂ ተራ እንተነበሮ፡ ነዚ ኣብ ልዕሊ ህዝቢ ኤርትራ ወሪዱ ዘሎ ሕሰም፡ ባህርያዊ ተፈጥሮ እዩ ኣበጊስዎ ዝበሃል ኣይኮነን። ግጉይ ፖሊሲታትን ፖለቲካዊ ውሳኔታትውን ኣብ ምግዳድ ናይ 'ቲ ጉዳይ ዓቢ ተራ ከም ዘለዎም ዘካትዕ ጉዳይ ኣይኮነን። ነዚ ጉዳይ ተገራጫዊ ዝገብሮ ድማ፡ እቲ ናይ ወጻኢ ሃገራት ሓገዝ ከምዘይቅበል ዝገልጽ ዝነበረ ስርዓት፡ ቀስ ብቐስ ኣብ ናይ ወጻኢ ናይ ረድኤት ሓገዝ ጽግዕተኛ ክኸውን ምብቅዑን፡ ብኣንጻሩ ድማ ነተን ዓለምለኻውያን ዘይመንግስታውያን ትካላት ነዚ መሰረታዊ ረድኤታዊ ሓገዝ ኣብ ምዝርጋሕ ንከይሳተፋ ምኽልካሉን እዩ።

እቲ ኣዝዩ ዘሕዝን ጎኒ ሕብረተ-ሰብና፡ እዚ ሕጂ ኣብ ሃገርና ኣጋጢሙ ዘሎ ማሕበራዊ ቅልውላው ማለት፡ ስቓይ ናይቶም ብዕድመ ዝደፍኡ ወለዲ እዩ። እዞም ኣረጋውያን ናይ ደቆም ሓልዮትን ክንክንን ኣብ ዝጽበይሉ እዋን፡ ነብሶም ባዕሎም ክኣልዩ ተፈሪድዎም ኣሎ። ብኣሽሓት ዝቑጸሩ ኤርትራውያን መንእሰያት ብምስምስ "ሃገራዊ ኣገልግሎት" ኣፍራዪ ዕድሚኦም ባኺኑ፡ ትምህርቲ ይኹን ሓዳር ከምኡ 'ውን ምንባይ ደቆም ከምዘይምልከቶም ተቐጺሩ፡ ስድራቤቶም ኣብ ግዜ እርጋኖም ንበይኖም ብዘይገለ ሓገዝ ሓዲጎም ኣብ ኣጻምእ ምድረ-በዳ ከርተት ክብሉን ኣብ ፈቐዶ ድፋዓት ተወሺጦም ግዜኦም ከባኽኑን ንርኢ ኣሎና። ካብኡ ሓሊፉ 'ውን ብኣሽሓት ዝቑጸሩ መንእሰያት ዶብ ሃገር ጥሒሶም ናብ ጎረባብቲ ሃገራት ይኹን ክንይኡ ሓሊፎም 'ውን ምድረ-በዳታት ሰንጢቖም ይስደዱ ምህላዎም፡ እቲ ናይ ላምፐዱሳ ህልቂት ብቑዕ ምስክርነት እዩ። እቶም ካብ ሃገር ክወጹ ዘይክኣሉን ወይ ውን ክወጹ ዘይደልዩን ድማ ህይወቶም ከም ንባርነት ዝተፈርዱ እሱራት ኮይኖም ተሪፎም ኣለዉ።

ኣብ ከተማታትን ገጠራትን ዝርከቡ እንዳ ድኳናት ብናይ ወጻኢ ኣቑሑት እዮም ተመሊኦም፡ ነዊሕ ሪጋ ምርኣይ ድማ መዓልታዊ ተርእዮ ኮይኑ ኣሎ። ህዝቢ ካብ ንግሆ ካብ ሰዓት 5 ኣትሒዙ ሪጋ ይስራዕ፡ ንነዊሕ ሰዓታት ድሕሪ ምጽባይ ድማ ባኒ ተወዲኡ ጽባሕ ምጹ ይበሃል። እተን ብብዝሒ ተማሃሮ ተጨናኒቐን ዝርከባ ኣብያተ ትምህርትታት እኹል መምሃሪ መጽሓፍትን ካልኦት ኣገደስቲ ናይ ትምህርቲ ንዋትን ከቕርባ ኣይከኣላን። እቶም መማህራን 'ውን ካብ ወርሒ ናብ ወርሒ ከሰጋግር ዝኽእል ክፍሊት ኣይወሃቦምን እዩ።. ጥዕናዊ ኣገልግሎት ኣዝዩ ሕማቅ ካብ ምኳኑ ዝተላዕለ እቶም ወሑዳት ዕድለኛታት ጥራሕ 'ዮም ንሕክምናዊ መርመራ ናብ ወጻኢ ክኸዱ ዝኽእሉ። እቲ ዘሕዝን ድማ፡ እዚ ዘይብቑዕ ሕክምናዊ ኣገልግሎት ኣብ'ታ ኣብ ግዜ ሓርነታዊ ቃልሲ ኣብ "ሓራ

መሬት" ኣብ ዝርከብ ስንጭሮታት ተኣምራት ከም ዝሰርሐት ዝንገረላ ንይትቲ ሃገርና የጋጥም ምህላዉ እዩ።

እቶም ኣብቲ መንግስቲ ዘለዉ ውፉያት ሃገራውያን፡ ነዚ ተስፋ ዘቑርጽ ኩነታት ብከመይ ክጻወርዎ ክኢሎም ንምምላሱ ከቢድ 'ዩ። ነቲ እንዳገደደ ዝኸይድ ዘሎ ብድሆታት ዓቕሞም ዝፈቕደሎም ግብረ-መልሲ ክህቡ ይፈትኑ 'ምበር እቲ ተስፋ ዘቑርጽ ኩነታት ከም 'ቲ ዝደልይዎ ንኽምክቱ ዕድል ዝህብ ኣይኮነን። ኩሉ ጻዕርታቶም - ኣብ ትሕቲ እቲ ካብ ቁጽጹሮም ወጻኢ ዝኾነ ግጉይ ፖሊሲታትን ፖለቲካዊ ውሳኔታትን ስለዘካይድዎ -ከምቲ ዝድለ ኣድማዒ ኣይኮነን። ዝኾነ ንፖሊሲታት ዝምልከት ሕቶ ይኹን ርእይቶ ወይ 'ውን ነቐፌታ ምሃብ ኣሉታዊ ሳዕቤናት ኣለዎ። እቲ ኣብ ልዕሊ ጉጅለ-15ን ጋዜጠኛታት ዝተወስደ ስጉምቲ ከም መጠንቀቕታ ንዝኾነ ይኹን ክመጽእ ዝኽል ተቓውሞ ኮይኑ፡ ተቓውሞታት ምስ ዝፍጠር ንምጭፍላቑ እቲ ሃገር ኣብ ትሕቲ ጥቡቕ ናይ ጸጥታ ምቁጽጻር ይርከብ ኣሎ። ከም 'ቲ ሓደ ኩብራረ ብዙሕ ዓይኒ እዩ ዘለዎ ዝብል ኣበሃህላ፡ ኩሉ ምንቅስቓሳት ናይ ህዝቢ ኣብ ትሕቲ ትዕዝብቲ ናይ 'ቲ መንግስቲ እዩ።

ኣብ ውሽጢ ሃገር ኄንካ ክግበር ዝኽእል ምንቅስቓስ ኣዝዩ ድሩት እዩ። ስለ ዝኾነ ድማ፡ ኤርትራ ኣዒንታ ናብቶም ኣብዚ ዝሓለፈ ዓሰርተ ዓመታት፡ ቁጽሮም ብዓሰርተታት ዕጽፊ እናወሰኸ ዝኸይድ ዘሎ ኣብ ወጻኢ ዝርከቡ ኤርትራውያን እዩ ዘማዕዱ ዘሎ።

እንታይ ክግበር ይግባእ

ብመሰረት ኣብ ላዕሊ ተጠቒሱ ዘሎ ፖለቲካውን ቁጠባውን ማሕበራውን ቅልውላው፡ እቲ ኣብ ናይ ነብሲ ወከፍና ኣእምሮ ዝመጽእ ሕቶ እንታይ ክግበር ኣለዎ ዝብል እዩ።

ሀ. ነዚ ተኸሲቱ ዘሎ ኣሰቃቒ ኩነታት ምእላይ ከድልየና እዩ።
ለ. ኣብ ተደጋጋሚ ናይ ጉድለታት ዓዘቕቲ ተሸኺልና ምስጓም ንከይንሸገር ድማ ካብ ድኽመታትና ተማሂርና ንቕድሚት ክንምርሽ ይግባእ።

ዝኾነ ነዚ ሕቶ ንምምላስ ዝግበር ፈተነታት ድማ ብኣድላይነት ሓድነት ክኣምን ይግባእ። ኣብ 11 ጥሪ 2009 ኣብ ለንደን ዓባይ ብሪጣንያ ኣብ ዝተኻየደ መስራቲ ጉባኤ ናይ ስድሪ (ዜጋታት ንዲሞክራሲያዊ መሰላት ኣብ ኤርትራ) መእተዊ ዘረባ ንክስምዕ ተዓዲመ ነይረ። ኣብ 'ቲ ኣጋጣሚ፡ ነቶም ነቲ ጉባኤ ንምድላው ተበግሶ ዝወሰዱ ሰባት ኣድናቖተይ ገሊጸ። ምምስራት ናይ 'ዚ ማሕበር ሓደ ካብቶም ኣብ ቃልሲ ኤርትራውያን ንምምስራት ዲሞክራስን

ልዕልና ሕግን እምነ-ኹርናዕ ዘንብር ምንቅስቓስ ምኳኑ ጠቒሱ ነይረ። ምስ ስድሪ ተመሳሳሊ ዕላማታት ዘለወን ብዙሓት ሲቪካውያን ማሕበራት ክቀላቐላ ምጅማረን ድማ፡ ነቲ ተስፋ ቖሪጹ ዝጸንሐ ኣብ ስደት ዝነብር ኤርትራዊ ሕብረተሰብ ተስፋ ዝህብን ዘተባብዕን ምኳኑ ጠቒሱ ምንባረይ ይዝክር።

ኣርእስቲ ናይ 'ታ ሽዑ ዘቕረብክዋ ጽሕፍቲ "ሓድነት ንዝዓበየ ዕላማን፡ ነጸብራቕ ናይ ሃገሩ ውድቀት ዘተሓሳሰቦ ኣቦውን" እያ ትብል ዝነበረት። ኣብታ ጽሕፍቲ ነቶም ተጋባእቲ፡ ከም ሓደ ካብ 'ቲ ናይ ንጡፍ ዕድመ ደረጃ ለጠቕ ናብ ዝበለ ናይ ንጥፈት ዕድመን፡ ናብ ዝበዝሐ ናይ ምንጽብራቕ ዕድመ ደረጃ ኣብ ዝተሰጋገርኩሉ እዋን፡ ንድሕሪት ተመሊሰ ዘሕለፍክዎ ህይወትን ሞያዊ ስራሕን ዘንጸባርቐሉ ግዜ ምኳኑ እየ ሓቢረዮም። ገለ ካብቶም ተሳተፍቲ ንርእይቶይ ምስ ሰምዑ ደንጽዮዎም (ብርግጽ ዕድመ ዝድርተኒ ዘይመስሎም ምንባሮም 'ውን ኣስተብሂለ)፡ እንተኾነ ግን፡ ናብ ናይ ሽምግልና ዕድመይ ኣብ ዝሰጋገረሉ ዘለኹ እዋን፡ ግዜ ይሕንበብ ከምዘሎ ተገንዚበ፡ ብዙሕ ከይተዓመመ ዝተረፈ ነገር ከምዘሎ 'ውን ኣስተብሂለ ናይ መወዳእታ መዕለቢኡ ክርእዮ ከም ዝደልን፡ ዝበዝሐ ክፋል ናይ ተሪፉኒ ዘሎ ዕድመ ድማ ኣብ ምዕዋት ናይ 'ዚ እነካይዶ ዘሎና ቃልሲ ከወፊ ድልው ምኳነይ እየ ሓቢረዮም"። ህዝብና ብሓደ ጨካን ውልቀ-መላኺ እንዳተጨፍለቐን ሃገርና ናብ ዕንወት ገጻ እንዳምርሐትን ከላ ድማ፡ ኣብ መንጎ ኤርትራውያን ስኒት ዘይምህላዉን፡ ፍልልያት 'ውን ይቕጽል ስለ ዘሎን ሐደ ካብ 'ቶም ክስራሓሎም ዝግባእ ዓበይቲ ዘይተወድኡ ዕማማት ምኳኑ ገሊጸ ነይረ። ድሮ 'ኳ ሓሙሽተ ዓመታት ቆጺሩ ገና እቲ ቀንዲ ጠንቂ ናይ ዘይምርድዳእን መወዳእታ ዘይብሉ ክትዓትን ኮይኑ ዘሎ፡ እቲ ንሃገርና ኣጋጢምዋ ዘሎ ሽግር ብኸመይ ንፍትሓዮ ዝብል ሕቶ ገና ኣብ ቦትኡ ኣሎ። እዚ ድማ ብኸመይ ለውጢ ነምጽእን ንህዝብና ድማ ብከመይ መንገዲ ካብዚ ኣጋጢምዎ ዘሎ ኣርዑት ጭቆና ነናግፎን ዝብል እዩ። ኣብዚ ክንግንዘቦ ዝግብኣና፡ እዚ ኣብ ሃገርና ዘሎ ቅልውላው ፍታሕ እንተዘይረኺቡ፡ ናብ ዕንወት ክመርሓና ምኳኑ ካብ ማንም ዝተሰወረ ኣይኮነን። ነዚ ኣጓኒፉ ዘሎ ሓደገኛ ዓይነት ተረኺቡ ኣብ ምፍታሕ ድማ ኣእምሮና ናብ ቅልጡፍ ፍታሕ ከነማእዝኖ ከድልየና እዩ። እቲ ናይ መጀመርታ ጠለብና እምበኣር ንኢሳይያስን ሰልፉን ዝልውጥ፡ ዲሞክራስያዊ ስርዓት ዝተክል ጥርኑፍ ሃገራዊ ግንባር ምምስራት ክኸውን ይግባእ። ኣብ ወጻኢ ዝርከቡ ብዙሓት ግዱሳት ኤርትራውያን ስሙር ግንባር ንምምስራትን ምውህሃድ ንምግባርን ዘይተሓለለ ጻዕርታት ኣካይዶም እዮም። ሃገርና ብሰሪ ሓደ ጨካን መራሕን ውሑዳት ተላኣኣኽቱን እንዳዓነወት እንከላ፡ ከም ሕብረተሰብ ክንፈላለ ኣይግባእን ብምባል ድማ ኣገዳስነት ናይዚ ስሙር ግንባር ኩሉ ሰብ ተረዲእዎ ኣሎ።

እታ ቀዳመይቲ ናይተን ክልተ ዛዕባታት

ጻዕርታትና ከነዋሃህድ ኣብ እንህቅነሉ እዋን፡ ኣብ ክልተ ዝተፈላለያን ኣብ ነንሕድሕደን ዝጸላለዋን ዛዕባታት ክንረዳዳእ ይግባኣና። እቲ ቀዳማይ፡ ሓድነት ናይ 'ቲ ነቲ ስርዓት ንክኣሊ ዝወሰነ ጥሙር ግንባር ምምስራት ኣገዳሲ እዩ። እቲ ካልኣይ ድማ፡ ነተን ድሕሪ ምእላይ ስርዓት ኢሳይያስ ሕበረ-ሰልፋዊ ዝኾነ ዲሞክራስያዊ ስርዓት ንክምስርታ ዝነጥፋ ዝተፈላለያ ፖለቲካዊ ሰልፍታት ምዕቃብን ምኹስካስን ይኸውን። ነቲ ናይ መጀመርታ ዛዕባ ንምትግባር ኣብ እንብገሰሉ እዋን፡ ከጋጥሙና ዝኽእሉ ጸገማት ኣብ ግምት ምእታው ኣገዳስነት ኣለዎ። እቲ ኣብ መንጎ 'ተን ዝተፈላለያ ጉጅለታት- ፖለቲካውያን ሰልፍታት ይኹን ሲቪላውያን ማሕበራት - ክፍጠር ዝኽእል ፋይዳ ዘይብሉ ክርክራትን ምትህልላኽን ኣሊና፡ ነቲ ስርዓት ንምልዋጥ ኣብ ዘኽእል ናይ ሓባር ዕላማ ንክንሰርሕ ኣብ 'ቲ ናብኡ ከብጽሓና ዝኽእል ናይ ስሙር ግንባር መንገዲ እምነት ከነንብር ይግባእ። ነዚ ሕቶ ብኣዎንታ ክንምልሶ ንኽእል ኢና ዝብል እምንቶ ድማ ኣሎኒ። ለውጢ ብሓደ ሞሎኮታዊ ሓይሊ ክመጽእ ይኽእል እዩ ኢልና ኣይንጽበን ኢና፡ ነዘን ዝተፈላለያ ጉጅለታት ናብ ሓደ ናይ ስሙር ግንባር መንገዲ መሪሕና ከም ዝቃለሳ ምግባር ድማ ዓቢ ትርጉም ኣለዎ።

ነዚ ከምዚ ዓይነት ነገር ዕውት ንምግባር ናይ ስድሪ ኣብነት ክንወስድ ንኽእል። ኣብቲ ጽሑፈይ ዘቅረብክሉ እዋን ይኹን ብድሕሪኡ፡ ስድሪ ነቶም ኣብ ዝተፈላለዩ ጉጅለታት ፋሕ ኢሎም ዘለዉ ኤርትራውያን ክጥርንፍ ዝኽእል ሓድነታዊ ሓይሊ ክኸውን ይኽእል ዶ ኢለ ሓቲተ ነይረ። እዚ ግን ንስድሪ ጥራሕ ዝምልከት ኣይኮነን፡ ነተን ካልኦት ስቪካውያን ማሕበራት ከም በዓል ዓለምለኻዊ ስምረት ኤርትራውያን (EGS) 'ውን ዝምልከት እዩ። ካልኦት ኣነ ዘይፈለጥክወን ከም ስድሪን ዓለምለኻዊ ስምረት ኤርትራውያን ዝኣመሰላ ሲቪካውያን ማሕበራት 'ውን ክህልዋ ይኽእላ። ከምዚ ኣነ ኣብ 2009 ዝበጻሕክዎ መደምደምታ፡ ዝኾነ ሰብ ነዞም መራሕቲ ናይዘን ሲቪካውያን ማሕበራት፡ ነዚ ኣዳኒፉ ዘሎ ሕማቅ ማሕበራውን ፖለቲካውን ኩነታት ንምብዳህ ሓምቢሶም ክወጽዎ ዘኽእሎም እኹል ብቕዓትን ጽንዓትን ብልሕን ኣለዎም ኢሉ ክግምት ይኽእል ይኸውን።

ናይ ዝሓለፉ ናይ ቀረባ ዓመታት ናይ ኤርትራውያን ውድባት ተሞክሮ ከምዘረጋገጾልና ግን፡ ኩለን ፖለቲካውያን ይኹና ሲቪካውያን ማሕበራት ተፈናጪለን ተወሰኽቲ ሓደስቲ ውድባት ክምስርታ ምርኣየን 'ዩ። ናይ 'ዚ ናይ ምፍንጫል ኩነት ንምርዳእ ታሪኻዊ ኣመዓባብልኡ ምፍታሽ ኣገዳሲ እዩ። ከምቲ ኣብ ላዕሊ ተጠቒሱ ዘሎ፡ ኣብ መወዳእታ 90ታትን ኣብ መጀመርታ 2000፡ ድሕሪ 'ቲ ብጉጅለ-15 ዝቐረበ ናይ ለውጢ ጠለብ ሓድሽ ናይ ተስፋ ብርሃን

ክቀላቐልል ጀሚሩ ነበረ። ምስ ምምስራት ሓደስቲ ሰልፍታትን ምብርባር ናይ 'ተን ናይ ተጋድሎ ሓርነት ኤርትራ መበቆል ዘለወን ውድባትን ድማ፡ እቲ ናይ ለውጥን ምሕዳስን ተስፋ መመሊሱ እናተኾልዐ መጺኡ። ስዒቡ 'ውን፡ ድሕሪ ናይ ነዊሕ ዓመታትን ኣድካምን ኣህላኽን ጉዕዞ፡ ነቲ ኣብ መንጎ 'ተን ዝተፈላለያ ፖለቲካውያን ሰልፍታትን ጉጅለታትን ዝነበረ ሃይማኖታዊ ይኹን ቀቢላውን ጉጅለኣውን ፍልልያት ብምውጋድ ብሓባር ንክሰርሓ ናይ ኤርትራዊ ዲሞክራስያዊ ኪዳን (ኤዲኪ) መስራቲ ጉባኤ ተኻይዱ። እቲ ናይ መወዳእታን ኣገዳስን ኣብ ኣዋሳ ኣብ ኢትዮጵያ ዝተኻየደ ኣኼባ፡ ንኹሉ ፍልልያት ኣወጊዱ ኣብቶም ኣገደስቲ ዝኾኑ ናይ ሃገራዊ ሓድነት ሕቶታትን ኣብ ካልኦት ኣገደስቲ ዝኾኑ ዛዕባታትን ኣብ ምርድዳእ በጺሑ ብሓባር ክስርሕ ዘኽእል ባይቶ ምምስራቱ ዝዝከር 'ዩ። ኣብ 'ዚ እዋን 'ዚ እቲ ናይ ህዝባዊ ግንባር ድሕረባይታ ዝነበሮ ሰልፊ ዲሞክራሲ ኤርትራ ምስ 'ቲ ናይ ተጋድሎ ሓርነት ኤርትራ ክፉል ዝኾነ ሰውራዊ ባይቶ ብምጽንባር ዝፈላልዮም ዝነበረ ታሪኻዊ ፍልልያት ኣለልዮም ኣብ ሓደ ብምጽንባር ሰልፊ ዲሞክራሲ ህዝቢ ኤርትራ (ሰዲህኤ) መስሪቶም።

እቲ ካልኣይ ዛዕባ፡ ሓድነትን ብዙሕነትን

ሃገራዊ ሓድነት ቀዳምነት ሂብና ኣብ እንጽውዓሉ ዘሎና እዋን /ሕጋውን ግቡእን ስለ ዝኾነ/፡ ኣረጋጊጸም ካብዘይምስትውዓል ገለ ገለ ሰባት ነዚ ሓድነት ንምምጻእ ዝግበር ቃልሲ፡ ዋላኳ እቲ ሓድነት ነዚ ዘሎ ስርዓት ኣብ ምእላይ ኣገዳስነቱ ዕዙዝ ምኳኑ እንተኣመኑ፡ ነቲ ስርዓት ኣሊና ንዕኡ ዝመስል ካልእ ዲክታቶርያዊ ስርዓት ንከይንተክል ስግኣቶም ይገልጹ 'ዮም። እዚ ድማ ቅቡል ስክፍታ 'ዩ። እዚ ካብ 'ቲ ከም ኣብ ግብጺ ድሕሪ "ዓረባዊ ሰውራ" ዘጋጠመ ዘይተደላዩ ኩነታት ንከይፍጠር ካብ ዝብል ስክፍታ ዝነቐለ 'ዩ።፡ ብዙሓት ሰውራታት 'ውን ምልካውያን መንግስታት ገልቢጠን ናታተን ሓደስቲ ምልካውያን ስርዓታት ከምዝመስረታ ታሪኽ ይምህረና እዩ። መልሲ ናይዚ ቅቡል ዝኾነ ስክፍታ እምበኣር፡ እተን ለውጢ ንምርግጋጽ ተባሂለን ሰሚረን ዝጸንሓ ሰልፍታት ይኹና ጉጅለታት ኣብቲ ድሕሪ ዓወት ዝምስረት ጥዕና ዘለዎ ፍልልያት ዘአንግድ ሕብረ-ሰልፋዊ ዲሞክራስያዊ ስርዓት፡ ነጻ ፖለቲካውያን ሰልፍታት ኮይነን ንክዋስኣ ነጻነት ንክህልወን ኣብቲ ናይ ሃገራዊ ስምረት ሓፈሻዊ ስምምዕ ክሰፍር ይግባእ። ከምዚ ዓይነት ሓፈሻዊ ስምምዕ ዝድለየሉ ምኽንያት ድማ፡ ምልካዊ ስርዓት ንካልኣይ ግዜ ከይምስረት ንምውሓስ እዩ። ነዚ ዝምልከት ንጹር ዝኾነ ስምምዕ ክህሉ ናይ ግድን እዩ። እቲ ከምዚ ዓይነት ስምምዕ ነቶም ናብቲ ትርጉም ዘለዎ ለውጢ ንምምጻእ ዝምስረት ሃገራዊ ስምረት ንከይጽንበሩ ዕጥይጥይ ዝብሉ ሰባት ኣብ ምትብባዕ ተራ ክህልዎ እዩ። እዚ ምቛም ናይ 'ዘን ዝጥመራ ሓደስቲ ሰልፍታት፡ ነቲ ኣንጻር ናይ 'ቲ

ፖለቲካውን ፋይናንስያውን ዲፕሎማስያውን ዓቕሚ ናይታ ሃገር ገቢቱ ዝርከብ ጨካን ስርዓት ኣብ ምውዳቕን ነቲ ናይ ተቓውሞ ደምበ ፖለቲካ ኣብ ምስማርን መሪሕ ተርኡ ከምዝጻወት ድማ ትስፉው እየ።

እቲ ናይ ምዕዋት ተኽእሎ ነቲ ኣብ ቅድሜና ዘሎ ብድሆታት ብከመይ መንገዲ ከም እንገጥሞ ብምንጽጻር ጥራሕ እዩ ክርአ ዝግባእ። ሓደ ካብቶም ንደምበ ተቓውሞ ዓቢ ማሕለኻ ኮይኑ ዘሎ፡ እቲ ኣብ መንጎ መንግስቲ ህግደፍን መንግስቲ ሱዳንን ዘሎ ምሕዝነት እዩ። ከም ሳዕቤን ናይ ‘ዚ ዘይቅዱስ ኪዳን ድማ፡ ገለ ኤርትራውያን ስደተኛታት ብሓይሊ ናብ ሃገሮም ከምለሱ ከለዉ፡ ኣብ ካርቱም ዝነበረ ቤት ጽሕፈታት ናይ ደምበ ተቓውሞ ‘ውን ተዓጽዩ ይርከብ። ብሰሪ እዚ ድማ፡ ኩለን እተን ውድባት ዋላ ‘ውን እተን ቅድሚ ሕጂ ኣብ ኣዲስ ኣበባ ቤት-ጽሕፈት ክኸፍታ ዘይደልያ ዝነበራ ሰልፍታት፡ ኣብ ኢትዮጵያ ቤት-ጸሕፈት ክኸፍታ ተገዲደን ኣለዋ። እቶም ነቲ ውድዓዊ ኩነታት ተቐቢሎም ንፖለቲካዊ ጽልውኡ ብተግባራዊ ውጽኢቱ ክገጥምዎ ዝደልዩ ነቲ ቤት-ጸሕፈት ኣብ ኣዲስ ኣበባ ምኽፋት ከም ሓደ ምቹእ ጉዳይ ክርእይዎ ከለዉ፡ እቶም ን“ወያነ ” ብዝተፈላለየ ምኽንያት ዝጸልኡን፡ ነቲ (ናይ ዓባይ ትግራይ) ዝብል ናይ መጻኢ ሕልሚ ኣለዎም ኢሎም ዝጥርጥሩን ግን ነቲ ኣብ ኣዲስ ኣበባ ቤትጽሕፈት ምኽፋት ዝብል ኣረኣእያ ኣይተቐበልዎን። እዚ ምስ መንግስቲ ኢትዮጵያ ክህሉ ብዛዕባ ዝግባእ ርክብ ብዝምልከት ተፈጢሪ ዘሎ ፍልልያት ነጸብራቕ ናይ ‘ቲ እናተሓላለኸ ዝመጸ ናይ ኤርትራን ናይ ዞባናን ፖለቲካ እዩ። . እቲ ብድሕሪ ምዝዛም ዶባዊ ኲናት ዝርአ ዘሎ “ኣይሰላም- ኣይኲናት” ኩነታትን፡ ናይ ኢትዮጵያ ንገለ ናይ ኤርትራ ቦታ ሒዛ ምህላዋን ድማ ነቲ ጉዳይ መሊሱ ሓላሊኽዎ ኣሎ።

ቀጻሊ ፍታሕ ናይ ምንዳይ ጻዕርታት

እንታይ እዩ ክግበር ዘለዎ ? ናይ ዝበዝሐ ህዝቢ ኤርትራ ድሌት ስርዓት ኢሳይያስ ካብ ስልጣን ተኣልዩ፡ ነቲ ዝፈጸሞ ገበናት ኣብ ፍርዲ ቀሪቡ ክሕተት ምግባር እዩ። ብዙሓት ኣባላት ፖለቲካውያን ሰልፍታትን ውልቀ ሰባትን ነዚ ዒላማ ንምውቃዕ ኣድላዪ ዘበለ ክገብሩ ጸኒሖም ኣለዉ። እንተኾነ ግን እቲ ጻዕርታት ከንቱ ኮይኑ እዩ ተሪፉ። ኣብ ‘ቲ ክካየድ ዝጸንሐ ቃልሲ እቲ ቀንዲ መካታዒ ነጥቢ ኮይኑ ዝጸንሐ ጉዳይ፡ ንኣገባብ ቃልሲ ዝምልከት - ማለት ብሰላማዊ መንገዲ ዶ ወይስ ብጎነጻዊ መንገዲ - ዝብል እዩ። እቲ ናይ ክልተ ወለዶታት እዋን ኣብ ብረታዊ ቃልሲ ዘሕለፈን ከቢድ ሰብኣውን ንዋታውን ዋጋ ዝኸፈለ ህዝቢ ኤርትራ፡ መብዛሕትኡ ብዕጥቃዊ ቃልሲ ጌርካ ለውጢ ምምጻእ ዝቕበሎ ኣይኮነን። እቶም ዕጥቃዊ ቃልሲ ዝኣምኑ ሰባት፡ ነቶም ለውጢ ብሰላማዊ መንገዲ ክመጽእ ይኽእል ኢሎም ዝኣምኑ እቲ ለውጢ ብከመይ

ኣገባብ ክመጽእ ከም ዝኽእል ሕቶ ምስ ቀረቡሎም፡ እቲ ኣብ ውሽጢ ሃገር ዘሎ ህዝቢ ብኹሉ ዝከኣል ዓይነት መንገዲ ምውዳብ እቲ ቀዳማይ ዕማም ኮይኑ፡ እቲ ካልኣይ ክማላእ ዘለዎ ጉዳይ ድማ ካብ ጎረባብቲ ሃገራት ዲፕሎማስያዊ ሓገዛት ምጥላብ፡ ብፍላይ ድማ ካብ 'ታ ጎረቤት ሃገር ዝኾነት ኢትዮጵያ ኣድላዪ ምኳኑ ጸቒጦም ይዛረቡሉ።

ነዚ ኣካራኻሪ ጉዳይ ብዝምልከት ኣብ መንጎ ፖለቲካውያን ሰልፍታት ክከየድ ዝጸንሐ ክትዕ፡ ኣብ ሓደ መደምደምታ ኣይበጽሐን። እተን ዝተፈላለያ ናይ ተቓውሞ ፖለቲካውያን ሰልፍታት ኣብ ሓደ ከረዳድኣን ዝኽእል ናይ ሓባር ዲፕሎማስያዊ ስትራተጂ ኣይበጸሓን። ዝተፈላለያ ሲቪካውያን ማሕበራትን ገለ ወነንቲ መርበብ ሓበሬታታትን ድማ ነዚ ጉዳይ ናብ ቅድሚት ንምድራኽ፡ ነዚ ኣርእስቲ ዝምልከት ቃለ-ምልልሳትን ናይ ጸሑፍ ዓንቀጻትን ኣኣንጊደን እየን። ከም ትዕዝብተይ፡ መብዛሕትኡ እቲ ለውጢ ብሰላማዊ ኣገባብ ክመጽእ ዝመርጽ ይመስለኒ፡ ገለ ውሑዳት 'ውን እቲ ጉዳይ ክፉት ተገዲፉ፡ ነቲ ወተሃደራዊ ኣገባብ ከም ኣማራጺ ክንጸግ የብሉን ዝብል ርእይቶ ዘለዎም 'ውን ኣለዉ።

እቲ ሰላማዊ ኣገባብ እቲ ዝተመረጸ ኣገባብ እዩ ኢልና እንተኣሚና፡ እቶም ከምኡ ኢልና እንሓስብ፡ ነዚ ኣገባብ ከዐውት ዝኽእል ናይ ሓባር ዲፕሎማስያዊ ስትራተጂ ክንነድፍን፡ ነቲ ኣብ ውሽጢ ዘሎ ህዝብና ክንውድብን ሓላፍነት ኣለና። እዚ ብጉጅለ መድረኽ ተወሲዱ ዘሎ ናይ ፈነወ ረድዮ ተበግሶ ተስፋ ዝህብ ኮይኑ፡ ከም ማእከል ናይ ምውህሃድን ጎስጓስን ብምኳን ነቲ ብወዲ ቫካሮ ተወሲዱ ዘሎ ተበግሶ ናብ ሓደ ህዝባዊ ምንቅስቓስ ክጥርንፍን፡ ተወሃሂዱ ነቲ ተቓውሞ ናብ ውሽጢ ሃገር ከምዝኣቱ ኣብ ምግባር ደራኺ ተራ ኣለዎ። እቲ ከነወግዶ ዘሎና ድማ እቲ ኣብ መንጎ ዝተፈላለያ ናይ ተቓውሞ ሓይልታት ዘሎ ዘይተደላዪ ምውድዳር እዩ።

ጣዕሳ፡ ምንጻህን ካሕሳን

ካብ 'ዞም ኣብ ላዕሊ ዝተጠቐሱ ኣማራጺታት ወጻኢ ዘሎ ካልእ ኣማራጺ ድማ ሃገራዊ ዕርቂ እዩ። እቲ ኣብዚ ናይ ታሪኽ መላግቦ ኣብ ሓደጋ ወዲቑ ዘሎ ጉዳይ እንታይ ምኳኑ ብንጹር ኣለሊና ክንፈልጦ ይግባእ። ነታ "ዝቖሰለት ሃገር" እትብል መጽሓፈይ ንክጽሕፍ ኣብ ዝገበርክዎ መጽናዕቲ፡ ዝተረዳእክዎ ነገር እንተ ነይሩ፡ ኣብ ግዜ ብረታዊ ቃልሲ - ኣብ ውሽጢ እቲ ክቡር ዕላማ - ምስቲ ኩሉ ዝተራእየ ጅግንነት ብዘሓት ሕማቓት ነገራት ከምዝተፈጸሙ እየ ኣስተብሂለ። ሃገርና ካብቲ ኣብ ግዜ ብረታዊ ቃልሲ ዝወረዳ ቁስሊ ክትፍወስ ይግባእ። እቲ ናይ ምፍዋስ መስርሕ ዝጅመር ድማ፡ ብቐዳምነት ንሕና ኣካል ናይ 'ታ ዝቖሰለት ሃገር ምኳና ምስ ተቐበልና እዩ። ኣብዚ ነዊሕ ናይ ምፍዋስ

መስርሕ እንንዓዘሉ እዋን ድማ ኣድላዪ ዘበለ ፍልጠት ንኽንድልብ ሓገዝ ከድልየና እዩ። ዘይተፈወሰ ቁስሊ ከምዘሎና ምእማን ግን ኣድላዪ ቅድመ-ኩነት እዩ። ኣብ 'ቲ ሃገራዊ ዕርቂ እንተኾነውን፡ ቁስልኻ ምእማን ሓደ ኣገዳሲ ቅድመ ኩነት እዩ። ገለ ሰባት እቲ ጉዳይ ብግልብጥ ክኸውን ይግብኦ ዝብል ስነ-ሞጎት ከቕርቡ ይኽእሉ። እዚ ማለት ድማ እቲ ምፍዋስ ኣብ መስርሕ ሃገራዊ ዕርቂ ዝርከብ ውጽኢት እዩ ይብሉ። እቲ ሕቶ፡ እቲ ሃገራዊ ዕርቂ ነቲ ብኢሳይያስ ዝተፈጸመ ታሪኻዊ ገበናት ንጎኒ ገዲፉ ክካየድ ይኽእልዶ ዝብል እዩ። ኢሳይያስ ንበይኑ ጥራይ ድማ ኣይኮነን ገበነኛ። ነቲ ምስ'ዚ ጉዳይ ዝተተሓሓዘ ዝተሓላለኸ ነገራት ኣብ ግምት ኣእትየ፡ ምስ ብዙሓት ሰባት ኣብ ዝገበርክዎ ምይይጥ ካብ ዝረኸብክዎ ሓሳባት፡ ንኢሳይያስ ናብ ፍርዲ ናይ ምቕራብ ሕቶ ድሕሪ እዚ ዘሎ ስርዓት ካብ ስልጣን ምእላዩን ሓደ ቅዋማውን ደሞክራስያውን መንግስቲ ምትካሉን ዝካየድ ጉዳይ ምዃኑ ይገልጹ። እዚ ድማ ንገዛእ ርእሱ ካልእ ሓሸውየ እዩ።

መጽናዕቲ ገበናዊ ክስን ፍርድን ዝምልከት ሕቶ ንጎድኒ ገዲፍካ፡ ዳርጋ ኩለን ፖለቲካውያን ሰልፍታት ነዚ ቆሲሉ ዘሎ ናይ ኤርትራ ፖለቲካዊ ኩነታት ንምፍዋስ ዘኽእል፡ ዲሞክራስያዊ ለውጥን ልዕልና ሕግን ሰብኣዊ መሰላት ዘኽብርን ቅዋማዊ መንግስቲ ምትካል ዝምልከት ዓንቀጻት ኣብ ፖለቲካዊ ፕሮግራማተን ኣስፊረንኦ ኣለዋ። ሙብዛሕትኡ ምስ 'ዚ ፖለቲካዊ ሕንጻጻት ክሰማማዕ ዝኽእል እኳ እንተ ኾነ ሓደ ክስገር ዘይክእል ሕቶ ግን ኣሎ፡ ንሱ ድማ እዚ ፖለቲካዊ መደባት ብኸመይ ኣብ ባይታ ይትግበር ዝብል ነጥቢ እዩ። ነዚ ሕቶ ኣብ እንምልሰሉ እዋን፡ ዋላኳ እደጋግም እሃሉ 'ምበር፡ ብዛዕባ እዚ ጉዳይ ንጹር ዝኾነ ርድኢት ክህልወና ይግባእ። ንሱ ድማ ኣብ ውሽጢ ኤርትራ ፖለቲካዊ ምንቅስቓስ ከይተመስረተ፡ ለውጢ ክመጽእ ኣይክእልን እዩ።

ምስቲ ኣብ ሃገርና ኣጋጢሙ ዘሎ ናይ ምዝራብን ምእካብን መሰላት ግህሰት፡ እቲ መንግስቲ ነቲ ህዝቢ በቲ ጨፍላቒ ናይ ጸጥታ ትካላቱ ኣቢሉ ዓፊኑ ሒዝዎ ክሳብ ዘሎ፡ ኣብ ውሽጢ ኤርትራ ፖለቲካዊ ምንቅስቓስ ክጅምር ኣይክኣልን እዩ እኳ እንተዘይተባህለ፡ እቲ ተኽእሎ ኣዝዩ ጸቢብ እዩ። እቲ ብወዲ ዓሊ ዝተገበረ ፈተነ ናይ "ፎርቶ" ዝምሃረና ነገር እንተ ሃልዩ፡ ክውደብን ክኹስከስን ዝኽእል ብውሽጢ ውሽጢ ዝኸይድ ዘይተወደበ ምንቅስቓስ ምህላዉ እዩ። ብኣጠቓላሊ፡ ኣብ ውሽጢ ሃገር ዝንቀሳቐስ ዝተዋሃሃደ ሃገራዊ ናይ ተቓውሞ ምንቅስቓስ ክህሉ እንተኾይኑ፡ ናይ ኣብ ወጻኢ ሃገር ዘሎና ኤርትራውያን ምትብባዕን ሓገዝን ክፍለዮ የብሉን። እቲ እዋናዊ ሕቶ እምበኣር፡ ነዚ ኩነታት ብከመይ ኣገባብ ኣብ ተግባር ከነውዕሎ ይግባእ ዝብል ሕቶ ምምላስ ይኸውን።

ኣብዚ ቀረባ እዋን፡ ብገለ ናእሽቱ ኤርትራውያን ምሁራት ዝቐረበ ሓሳብ ኣሎ። ንምጥቃሱ ዝኣክል፡ እዞም ምሁራት እቲ ለውጢ ነቲ ስርዓት ብምዕላው ዘይኮነ፡ ካብ ውሽጢ ንመራሕቲ መንግስቲ ኤርትራን ውድቦምን ኣብታ ሃገር ፖለቲካዊ ለውጢ ንኸምጽኡ ግቡእ ጠለባት ብምቕራብ ለውጢ ክመጽእ ይኽእል እዩ ዝብል እምነት ኣለዎም። ነዚ ንምዕዋት፡ ንላዕለዎት መራሕቲ መንግስቲ፡ ማለት ንካቢነ ሚኒስተራትን ናብ ላዕለዎት ኣባላት ውድብን ዝበጽሕ ደብዳቤ ጽሒፎም። እዚ ደብዳቤ ድሕሪ ናይ ላምፐዱሳ ህልቂት ዝተዳለወ ኮይኑ፡ ልዙብ ዲፕሎማስያዊ ቋንቃ ዝሓዘለንን ነቶም መራሕቲ ድማ ንዲሞክራስያዊ ለውጢ ከም ዝኣምኑ ብምሕሳብ ተዳልዩ ዝተጻሕፈን እዩ ነይሩ። እቲ ደብዳቤ፡ ንኣረኣእያ ናይ መብዛሕትኦም ኣብ ደምበ ተቓውሞ ዘለዉ ኤርትራውያን ኣየንጸባርቕን እዩ። ኣብቲ ኢሳይያስ ኣብ ግዜ ቃልሲ ፈጺምዎም ዝብሃል ገበናት ሓደ ዓይነት ኣራኣእያ ዘለዎም ኣይመስለን። ዋላኳ እዞም ትስፉዋት ምሁራት ካብቲ ዘለዎም ሰናይ ድልየት ተበጊሶም ንኢሳይያስን ስርዓቱን እቲ ቅኑዕ ኮይኑ ዝተሰምየም ሓሳባት ከቕርቡ መሰሎም እንተኾነ፡ ኢሳይያስ ንከምዚ ዓይነት ጠለባት ሰሚዑ መንገዱ ከማዓራሪ እዩ ኢልካ ምሕሳብ የዋህነት ጥራይ እዩ። ብካልእ መንገዲ ድማ፡ ንኢሳይያስ ነቲ ዝፈጸሞ ገበናት ተሓታቲ ምኳኑን፡ ኣብ ፍርዲ ክቐርብ ዝግብኦ ምኳኑዝጠልቡ ብዙሓት ኣኼባታት ተኻይዶምን ብዙሓት ጽሑፋት ድማ ኣብ ናይ ተቓውሞ መርበብ ሓበሬታታት ተዘርጊሖም እዮም። ኣብ 'ዚ ቀረባ እዋን፡ ኣብ ዋሽንግተን ዲሲ ብዓለምለኻዊ ስምረት ኤርትራ ዝተዳለወ ኣኼባ፡ ሓደ ናይ ፖለቲካዊ ሳይንስ ፕሮፌሰር ሓንቲ መጽናዕታዊት ጽሕፍቲ ኣቕሪቡ ነይሩ። እቲ ተበግሶ ናይ 'ዚ ምሁር ፡ ንኢሳይያስ ናብ ፍርዲ ንምቕራብ ዝሰርሕ ህዝባዊ ምንቅስቓስ ምጅማር እዩ ነይሩ።

ጉዳይ ኣብ ወጻኢ ዝነብር ህዝብናን ጉዳይ ስደተኛታትን

ኣብ 'ዚ እዋን፡ ኣብ ወጻኢ ዝነብር ዘሎ ተቓዋሚ ህዝብና ነቶም ኣብ ወጻኢ፡ ኣብ ኣውሮፓን ኣሜሪካን ኣብ ካልኦት ክፍላተ-ዓለማትን ዝነብሩ ስደተኛታት ኤርትራውያን ኣጋጢምዎም ንዘሎ ሽግራት ቅልጡፍ መፍትሒ ክረኽበሎም ይግባእ። ኣብዚ ቀረባ እዋን፡ ነዚ ንስደተኛታት ዘጋጥሞም ዘሎ ጸገማት ከም ኣርእስቲ ኣልዒለ ብኸመይ መንገዲ ሓባራዊ ፍታሕ ከነናድየሎም ከም እንኽእል ሓሳባት ንምርካብ ምስ ገለ ኤርትራውያን ማሓዙተይ ተዛትየ ኔረ።

ነቲ ጉዳይ "ኤርትራ ናበይ" ብዝብል ሕቶኣዊ ኣርእስቲ እየ ኣበጊሰዮ። ነዚ ሕቶ ብምንቃለይን ዝመስለኒ ሐሳባት ብምፍሳሰይን፡ ንማንም ሰልፊ ይኹን ጉጅለ ከም ዘይውክል ከነጽር እደሊ። እዚ ኮይኑ ግን፡ ናይ ኤርትራ ፖለቲካውያን ሰልፍታት ይኹና ሲቪካውያን ማሕበራት ኣብ ኩሉ ዘካይድኦ ንጥፈታት ሞሉእ ደገፊይ ከምዘይፍለየን ክሕብር እፈቱ። ብካልእ ሸነኽ ድማ ደምበ ተቓውሞ

ካብቲ ናይ ምትህልላኽ መንፈስ ወጺኡ፡ ብሓድሽ ሃገራዊ መንፈስ ዝተመልአ ሓድነት መስሪቱ ነታ ሃገር ናይ ምድሓን ሓላፍነት ክሰከም እምሕጸን። ኣብዚ እዋን፡ ከም ብሓድሽ ክሓስቡን ኣድማዕን ስሙርን ተቓውሞ ንክምስርቱ ክሰርሑ ይግባእ። በዚ ሃገራዊ መንፈስን ብሓድነትን ጥራይ እዮም ድማ ኣንጻር ህግደፍ ናብ ዓወት ክመርሑና ዝኽሉ። እዚ ኣብ ላዕሊ ዝጠቐስክዎ ነጥብታት፡ ንናይ ደምበ ተቓውሞ ፖለቲካ ንጥፈታት ንልዕሊ ዓሰርተ ዓመታት ብምክትታልን ብምምርማርን ዝኣከብክዎ መርትዖታት ምርኩስ ጌረ ዝበጻሕክዎ መደምደምታ 'ዩ። ዋላኳ ሓድሽ ዝቀላቐል ተስፉ ዝህብ ናይ ሓባር ንጥፈታት ተበግሶታት እንተሃለወ፡ እዚ ግን ነቲ ኣብ ኤርትራ ክትከል ዝድለ ዘሎ ዲሞክራስያዊ ስርዓት ኣብ ምዕዋት ኣኻሊ ኣይኮነን።

ኣብ ኣሜሪካን ኣውሮጳን ብገለ ኣድማዒ ተራ ክጻወቱ ዝኽእሉ ዉፉያት ውልቀሰባት ዝምርሓ ብዙሓት ሰቪካውያን ማሕበራት ተመስሪተን ኣለዋ። እዘን ሲቪካውያን ማሕበራት ኣበርክቶኣን ዓቢ ይኹን 'ምበር ብዓይኒ ኣገዳስነት ናይ ስርዓት ምልዋጥ ወሲድካ ፡ ከም መተካእታ ናይ ፖለቲካውያን ውድባትን ሰልፍታትን ኮይነን ክንቀሳቐሳ ኣይግባእን። ተራ ናይ ሲቪካውያን ማሕበራት ምስ ናይ ፖለቲካውያን ውድባት ኣነጻጺርካ፡ እተን ሲቪላውያን ማሕበራት ብዝተኻእለ መጠን ኣብ ናይ ተሓጋጋዝነት ተራ ክሕጸራ ከም ዝግባእ ሓፈሻዊ ስምምዕ ክህሉ ይግባእ። ኣብ ገለ ገለ ተኣፋፊ እዋናት እዘን ሲቪካውያን ማሕበራት ካብ ሞራላዊ ሓላፍነት ተበጊሰን ንገለ ገለ ብመንግስቲ ወይ ውን ብውድባት ዝውሰድ ግጉይ ስጉምትታት ወይ 'ውን ክፍጸሙ እናተገብኦም ከይተፈጸሙ ዝስገሩ ኩነታት ተዓዚበን ነቲ መንግስቲ ይኹን ነቲ ማሕበር ክኹንና ሞራላዊ ሓላፍነት ክህልወን ይኽእል። ኣብ ትሕቲ ከም 'ዚ ዓይነት ኩነታት ናይ ክልቲኦም ረብሓታት ክጋጠም ይኽእል። እንተኾነ ግን እተን ፖለቲካውያን ማሕበራት፡ ዋላ 'ኳ እቲ ተግባራት ክኹነን ከምዝለዎ ዝድግፉ እንተኾና ብዓይኒ ዲፕሎማሲ ተመልኪተን መኸሰብ ዘይረኽባሉ ኮይኑ ምስ ዝረኣየን ስቕ ኢለን ክሓልፍኦ ዝመርጻሉ እዋን ኣሎ። ኣብ ከምዚ ዓይነት ኩነታት ድማ እቲ ነገር ኣብ መንጎ እተን ፖለቲካውያን ሰልፍታትን እተን ሲቪካውያን ማሕበራትን ፍልልያት የንጸባርቕ። ዝኾነ ኮይኑ፡ እዘን ሲቪካውያን ማሕበራት ንጥፈታተን ብኣድማዕነት ንክፍጽማ ብከስርሕ ዝኽእል ቅርጺ ክውደባን ክሓብራን ይግባእ። እዚ ስለዝኣምን ድማ እየ፡ ኣብ ናይ ስድሪ መስራቲ ጉባኤ ንክሳተፍ ንዝቐረበለይ ዕድመ ተቐቢለ፡ ብዘይ ገለ ምጥርጣራት ዝተቐበልኩዎ። ብተማሳሳሊ ምኽንያት ድማ እየ ነቲ ብዓለም-ለኻዊ ስምረት ኤርትራውያን ዝተገብረ ኣኼባታት ተሳቲፈ። ካብ ዓለምለኻዊ ስምረት ኤርትራውያን ድማ “ልሳን ልዕልና ሕጊ” ዝብል ሽልማት ምርካበይ የሐብነንን የኹርዓንን ጥራሕ ዘይኮነ፡ ክብርን ሓጎስን 'ውን ይስምዓኒ።

ኣብዚ ጸቒጠ ክጠቕሶ ዝደሊ ነገር እንተ ሃልዩ፡ እተን ሲቪካውያን ማሕበራት ንጹርን ዝተጠምረን ዕላማታትን ሽቶታትን ክህለወን ይግባእ። ነቲ ካብ ፖለቲካውያን ሰልፍታት ዝፈልየን ነጥብታት ብንጹር ፈሊጠን፡ ካብ ክፍጠር ዝኽእል ዘይምርድዳእን ግጭታትን ክርሕቃ ኣለወን። ተራ ፖለቲካውያን ሰልፍታትን ሲቪካውያን ማሕበራትን ነቲ ብስርዓት ህግደፍ ኣብ ልዕሊ ህዝብና ዝወርድ ዘሎ ምግሃስ ሰብኣዊ መሰላት ምቅላዕን ምቅዋምን ጥራሕ ዘይኮነ፡ ነቶም ካብ ትሕቲ ኣርዑት ናይ 'ቲ ስርዓት ሃዲሞም ዝመጹ ዘለዉ ስደተኛታት ንምሕጋዝ ምስራሕ 'ውን ከድሊ 'ዩ። ነዚ ኣብ ምዕዋት፡ መርበብ ሓበሬታታት ደምበ ተቓውሞ ዓቢ ተራ ኣለወን። እተን መርበብ ሓበሬታታት እንተኾና 'ውን ኣብ ናይ ሓባር ዕላማ ዝተመስረተ ንጹርን መሰረታውን ስምምዓት ከገብራን፡ ብሓባር ንምስራሕ ድማ ዘይተደላዩ ተጻብኦታትን ሓድሕዳዊ ምዝልላፍን ከወግዳ ይግባእ። ሓደ ካብ 'ቶም ክዕመሙ ዘለዎም ኣገደስቲ ሓባራዊ ስራሓት እምበኣር፡ ነዚ ሃገር ራሕሪሑ ናብ ስደት ዘምርሕ ዘሎ ስደተኛ፡ ንኽጣየስ ሓጊዝና፣ ኣንቂሕና፣ ወዲብና፣ ንለውጢ ከምዝሰርሕ ምግባር እዩ። እዘን ኣብ ናይ ተቓውሞ ደምበ ዘለዋ ውድባትን ስቪካውያን ማሕበራትን ድማ ነዚ ዕላማ'ዚ ኣብ ምዕዋት ቦኺረን ከምዘለዋ ተገንዚበን፡ ድኽመታተን ኣለልየን፡ ነዚ ናይ ስደተኛታት ዕቑር ሓይሊ ኣብ ደምበ ተቓውሞ ናይ ምስታፍ ጻዕርታት ብዝተዓጻጸፈ ደረጃ ክብ ንኽብል ዕማማተን ብተዓጻጻፊ ደረጃ ከዛይዳ ይግባእ።

እቲ ዝበዝሐ ክፋል ናይ 'ዞም ኣብ ወጻኢ ዝነብሩ ዘለዉ ኤርትራውያን፡ እቶም ኣብ ውሽጢ 'ዚ ዓሰርተ ዓመታት ሃገር ራሕሪሖም ዝወጹ እዮም። እቲ ካብ ሃገር ኣምሊጦም ንክወጹ ዘሕልፍዎ ናይ ጸበባ ዛንታ ንባዕሉ፡ ምስክርነት ናይ 'ቲ ናይ ኩሉ ኤርትራዊ መለለዪ ዝኾነ ባህሪ፡ ትብዓት፣ ዘይተጻዓድነትን፣ ተሪር መርገጽን ንሒን ኣስሓኮን ምኳኑ እዩ ዘነጽረልና። ገለ ውሑዳት ካብዞም ጀጋኑ ኣምሊጦም ዝመጹ፡ ኣብ 'ተን ሰልፍታትን ሲቪካውያን ማሕበራትን ተጸንቢሮም ይነጥፉ ኣለዉ። እቲ ዝበዝሐ ክፋል ግን፡ ነቲ ዘጓንፎ መዓልታዊ ናብራ ንክብድህ ኣብ ውልቃዊ ዋኒኑ ተሸኺሉ ነቲ ዝሓለፎ ስቓይ ረሲዑ ክነብር ዝመረጸ እዩ። ብዙሓት ነቲ ዝሓለፍዎ ዘስካሕክሕ ኩነታት ይኹን ንኤርትራ 'ውን ከይተረፈ ክዝክርዋ ከምዘይደልዩ ብስምዒት 'ዮም ዝገልጹ። ኣባላት ፖለቲካውያን ሰልፍታትን ሲቪካውያን ማሕበራትን ነዞም ስደተኛታት ክውድብዎም ኣብ ዝፍትኑሉ እዋን፡ እዞም መንእሰያት ንሃገሮም ልዕሊ ዝግብኦም ከምዘገልገሉ ብምጥቃስ፡ ብዛዕባ ሃገር ምስባኽን ምምጽዳቕን ደው ንከብልዎ ብትብዓት ይምልሱሎም፡ ተመሊሶም ኣብ ዓዶም ክነብሩ ዝደልዩ 'ውን ኣይመስሉን። በቲ ዘሕለፍዎ መሪር ታሪኽ ስለ ዝጎሃዩ ድማ ናብ ልቦም ተመሊሶም ሃገሮም ከም ዘገልግሉ ንምግባር ከቢድ ጻዕሪ ክሓተና እዩ። እዚ ድማ፡ ሓደ ካብቲ ኣዝዩ ዘሕዝን ክፋል ናይ ታሪኽና ኮይኑ፡ ኣብታ ጽባሕ

ክንሃንጻ እንደሊ ዘሎና መጻኢት ኤርትራ ከቢድ ጽልዋ ዘንብርን ኣብ ምቅላሱ ኣገደስቲ ሕቶታት ዘለዓዕልን ጉዳይ ኮይኑ ኣሎ።.

"እዚ 'ውን ክሓልፍ እዩ"

መንእሰያት ኤርትራ ሃገሮም ራሕሪሖም ናብ ወጻኢ ሃገራት ናብ ኣውሮፓን ሰሜን ኣሜሪካን የምርሑ ምህላዎም ርዱእ ኮይኑ፡ ብፍላይ ድሕሪ ናይ ላምፐዱሳ ህልቂት፡ እዚ ጉዳይ 'ዚ ካብ ተዋሂብዎ ዝጸንሐ ኣቓልቦ ንላዕሊ ጠመተ ክግበረሉ ይግባእ። እቲ ኣድህቦ ኣብ ክልተ ዝተኸፍለ ኮይኑ፡ እቲ ናይ ሓጺር እዋን ፍታሕ ነቶም ስደተኛት ብህጹጽ ዘድልዮም ነገራት ምምላእ ክኸውን እንከሎ፡ እቲ ካልእ ድማ ናይ ማእከላይን ነዊሕ ግዜ ፍታሕን ዝጠመተ ክኸውን ይግባእ። እቲ ናይ ነዊሕ ግዜ ፍታሕ ዘድልዮ ብናይ ፖለቲካ ወይ 'ውን ብናይ ስነ-ሕበረተሰብ ከምኡ 'ውን ብናይ ታሪኽ ክኢላታት ክካየድ ዝግብኦ ሰፊሕ መጸናዕቲ እዩ። እዚ ግን ነቶም ቅልጡፍ ፍታሕ ዝጽበዩ ዘለዉ ስደተኛታት ከም መጋየጽን ግዜ መባኸንን ጥራሕ እዩ። ኣብ 2009-2010 ዘካየድክዎ መጽናዕቲ፡ ብመሰረት ናይ ወንጌላውያን ቤተክርስትያን ሓበሬታ ኣርባዕተ ሽሕ ዝኾኑ ስደተኛታት (ናይ ሳዋ ስደተኛታት ኢለ ዝጽውዖም) ናብ 'ቲ ቤተክርስትያን ተጸንቢሮም ኣለዉ። እዚ ቤተ ክርስትያን 'ዚ ቁጽሪ ኣባላቱ እንዳዓበየ ይመጽእ ኣሎ። እቶም ኣመንቲ ወንጌላውያን ክርስትያናት ድማ ብዕላማ ዝምርሕሉ ህይወት ሃልይዎም፡ ይምሃሩን ጽቡቕ ስራሕ ይሰርሑን ቤተሰብ ይምስርቱን ኣለዉ። ካብተን ከም ብዓል ዓባይ ብሪጣንያ ዝኣመሰላ ዑቕባ ዝሓተቱለን ሃገራት ዝርከባ ኣሕዋት ወንጌላውያን ቤት ክርስትያናት ድማ ዝሓሸ ሓገዝ ክረኽቡ ዕድል ረኺቦም ኣለዉ። ንኣይ ከምዝመስለኒ ድማ ብፍላይ ተቓወምቲ ሲቪካውያን ማሕበራት፡ ነዞም ዝስደዱ ዘለዉ ኤርትራውያን እቲ ዝግብኦም ቦታ ብምሃብ፡ ኣብቲ ሃናጺ ንጥፈታት ንኽዋስኡ ብተገዳስነት ክሕዝኦም ይግባእ። እቲ መራሒ ዕላማ ንኩሉ ኤርትራዊ ብዘይ ናይ ሃይማኖትን ዞባን ቀቢላን ኣፈላላይ ኣብቲ ንህይወቶምን መጻኢ ዕድሎም ዝምልከት ውሳኔታት ከሳትፉ ይግባእ።

ኣብዚ ግዜ'ዚ፡ ንኤርትራውያን ዘጋጥሞም ዘሎ ጸገማት ከስተንትን ከለኹ፡ ነቲ ብስቓይ ዝተመልአ ድምጺ ናይ ግዳያት በደዊን ሲናይ ዝኾኑ ኤርትራውያን ክዝክሮ ይኽብደኒ። ቃላት ናይቶም ኩሊቶም ናብ ዕዳጋ ቅድሚ ምውራዱ፡ ዝተገርፉን ዝተሳቐዩን መንእሰያት ኣሕዋትና ብቐሊሉ ካብ ኣእምሮ ዝሕከኽ ኣይኮነን። ሞት ኣንጸላልይዎም ኮላሊቶም ካብ ኣካላቶም ተጠቢሑ እንዳተወስደ ከሎ ''እዚ እውን ክሓልፍ እዩ'' ዝብል ናይ ተስፋ ቃላት እዮም ዘውጽኡ ነይሮም። በቲ ኣብ ግዜ ሽግርን ጸበባን ዝረአ ዘይጸዓድ መንፈስ ኤርትራውያን ዝጠራጠር ሰብ እንተሃልዩ ድማ፡ ነዚ ክንዮ ሽግር ዝጥምት መንፈስ ናይዞም

ጀጋኑና ጽንዓት ክነዘኻኽሮ ይግባእ። ኩላትና ድማ፡ ነዚ ናይዞም ጀጋኑ መንእሰያት ኤርትራውያን ዘይጽዓድ መንፈስ እንዳዘከርና ኣብ ጉዕዞና ንመንፈሶም ዓቂብና ክንጎዓዝ ይግባእ።

ብዛዕባ 'ዞም ዝሳቐዩ ዘለዉ ኣሓትን ኣሕዋትን ፡ ኣብ ቀንዲ ድሌታቶም ኣድሂብና ኣነጺርና ክንሓስብን ነቲ ዘጋጥሞም ዘሎ ጸገማት ብኸመይ ፍታሕ ንረክብ ክንዘራረብን ኢሂን ምሂን ክንበሃሃልን ይግባእ። ነዚ ኣጋጢሙ ዘሎ ጸገማት ቢዲሆም ክሰግርዎን ንዕኡ ሰጊሮም ኣብቲ ሃገራዊ ዛዕባ እጃሞም ንከበርክቱ እንታይ ክግበር ይግባእ? እቲ ኣብዚ እዋን ብቀዳምነት ዝስራዕ ድማ ነዞም ኤርትራውያን ስደተኛታት ሓገዝን ምቹትን ምፍጣር ካብ ኮነ፡ ኩለን ሲቪካውያን ማሕበራት ኩሉ ክርከብ ዝኽእል ሓገዝ - ወግዓዊ ይኹን ዘይወግዓዊ - ተጠቒመን ኤርትራውያን ስደተኛታት ኣብ ምሕጋዝ ክነጥፉ ይግባእ። እቲ ኣብ 2008 ካብ ዝተፈላለያ ኤርትራውያን ጉጅለታት ዝተዋጸአ ሓይሊ ዕማም ጽቡቅ ተበግሶ እዩ። እቲ ብሓው ወዲ ቫካሮ ዝተወስደ ዝነኣድ ተበግሶ 'ውን ፖለቲካዊ ለውጢ ኣብ ምምጻእን ናብ ንዝተዘናበሉ ኤርትራውያን ስደተኛታት ዝረድእ ሲቪካዊ ተበግሶ ክሰጋገር ይግባእ። እቲ ኣብ እስራኤልን ኣብ ግብጺን ኣብ ዞባ ሲናይ ኣብ ልዕሊ ግዳያት ኤርትራውያን ስደተኛታት ዘጓንፍ ዘሎ ናይ መሰል ምግሃስ ገበናት ድማ ኣቓልቦ ክውሃቦን ስቓዮም ንምውዳእ ህጹጽ ፍታሕ ክግበረሉ ይግባእ።

ሓድሕድ ምፍልላጥ - ቀንዲ መትከል ህላውነት ሃገር

ከምቲ ኣብ ዝሓለፈ ክፋላት ዝተጠቕሰ፡ ንብድሕሪ ኢሳይያስ እትመጽእ ኤርትራ ጠሚትናን፡ ንእንሓልፎ ዘለና ጸገማት ኣብ ግምት ኣእቲናን ንውድዓዊ ኩነታትና ብከመይ ክንመርሕን ክንልውጥን ከም ዘሎና ንነብስና ክንሓትት ይግባእ። እቲ ብቀዳምነት ክመጽእ ዝግብኦ ዝዓበየ ሕቶ ግን፡ እቲ ንህላወ ናይ ሓንቲ ዝተፈላለዩ ኣባላት ሕብረተ-ሰብ ዝሓቆፈት ሃገር ዝመርሕን ንሓባራዊ ጥምረት ዘአንግድን ቅዋማዊ ንድፊ ምቕባል እዩ። ሓድሕድ ምፍልላጥ ከም ኣገዳሲ ምሕደራዊ መትከል ህላውነት ሃገር ክንቅበሎ ድማ ይግባእ። እንታይ ዓይነት ቅዋም ንቕበል ብዘየገድስ፡ ነዚ ቀዳማይ መትከል ክንነጽጎ ኣይንኽእል ኢና። ጀምስ ቱሊ ዝተባህለ ፍሉጥ ካናዳዊ ምሁር ከምዚ ክብል ጠቒሱ ኣሎ፡ "እቲ ናይ ዘበና ሕቶ ኮይኑ ዘሎ . . . . ሓደ ቅዋም ንሕጋዊ ጠለባት ናይ ነፍሲ-ወከፍ ኣባላት ዝተፈላለዩ ሕብረተሰባት ብዘዕግብ መንገዲ ክምልስ ይኽእልዶ፡ ክንዲ ዝኾነ ድማ ኩላቶም ብነጻ ፍቓድ ኣብ 'ቲ ቅዋማዊ ምትእኽኻብ ክጽንበሩ ይኽእሉ። ነዚ ድማ 'ናይ ሓድሕድ ምፍልላጥ' ንበሎ እሞ ቀጺልና ብዛዕባ ዝርዝራቱ ክንሓትት።"

ነዚ ጉዳይ ከም ዘለዎ ወሲድና፡ ኣብ ብዙሕነትና መንቅባት ከይህሉ ክንፍትሽ ኣድላዪ እዩ። ገለ ፈላለይቲ ሃጓፋት ኣለዉ ኢልና እንተ ኣሚና ድማ ነቶም ሃጓፋት ከነላግቦም ከንክእል ከንግደድ ኢና። እዘን ፖለቲካውያን ማሕበራት ንዘሎና ሃጓፍ ንምምላእን ንሃገራዊ ሓድነትና ንምዕቃብን እንታይ ክገብራ ይግብአን? ሃይማኖታውን ቀቢላውን ፍልልያት ሃጓፋት ተባሂሎም ክጥቀሱ ዝኽእሉ ኣለዉ ዶ?

እቲ መልሲ ኣወንታዊ እንተኾይኑ፡ ነዚ ፍልልያት ንምጽባብ ድልድል ምስራሕ ይክኣል ዶ? ካብ ሕሉፍ ተመክሮና፡ ንሃይማኖታዊ ፍልልያት ዝምልከት እንታይ ዓይነት ትምህርቲ ቀሲምና፡ ነዚ ንምትዕርራይ ከ ኣብቲ ዝህሉ ቅዋም እንታይ ዓይነት ዓንቀጻት ክህሉ ንደፍእ? እዘን ዘለዋ ፖለቲካውያን ይኹና ሲቪካውያን ማሕበራት ነዚ ጉዳይ ዝምልከት ፍታሕ ኣብ ምንዳይ ነጢፈን ይፈልጣ ዶ? እወ፡ ንብል እንተ'ኼና፡ ብኸመይ መንገዲ፡ እንታይ ዓይነት ወጽኢት ከ ተረኺቡ? ዝብሉ ሕቶታት ክለዓሉ ግድን እዩ። ነዚ ኣሎ ዝብሃል ሃጓፋት ብፍላይ ድማ ነቲ ምሕራም ናይ ገለ ኣካላት ሕብረ-ተሰብና ካብ ተሳታፍነት ናይ ሃገር ምምራሕን ካብ ተጠቃምነት ምምቕራሕ ቁጠባዊ ሃብቲ ሃገርን ዝምልከት ብዙሓት ናይ ዘይዕግበታት መግለጺታትን መርኣያታትን ጸኒሖም እዮም። ብመንጽር ጽልዋ ናይ 'ዚ ፖለቲካዊ ሃጓፋት ተጠሚቱ ኣብ ምምስራት ናይ ዝተፈላለያ ፖለቲካውያን ማሕበራት ዝተራእየ ኣወንታዊ ሽንኻት ዶ ይመዝን ወይስ ኣሉታዊ? እዚ ምምስራት ናይዘን ፖለቲካውያን ማሕበራት፡ ኣብ ትሕቲ መትከል ሓድነት ኣብ ውሽጢ ብዙሕነት ክጠቓለል ይኽእል ዶ?

ኩለን እዘን ፖለቲካውያን ማሕበራት፡ ዋላ እዘን ኣብ ቀረባ እዋን ዝተመስረታ ከም ብዓል መድረኽ ይኹና ካልኦት ተመሳሰልቲ ጉጅለታት ከይተረፉ፡ ናይ ሃገርናን ህዝብና ዝበለጸ ረብሓ ኣብ ልበን ዘቐመጣ ኮይነን፡ ነዚ ዘሎ ፍልልያት ኣብ ምጽባብ ክሕግዝ ዝኽእል ድልድል ኣብ ምህናጽ ሓገዘን ከበርክታ ይኽእላ እየን ዝብል ግምት ኣሎኒ። ነዚ ኣብ ሃገርና ኣጋጢሙ ዘሎ ፍልልያት ኣብ ምጽባብ ድማ፡ ምህናጽ ድልድልጥራሕ እዩ ፍታሕ ከምጽእ ዝኽእል ዝብል ጽኑዕ እምነት ኣሎኒ። እዚ ድልድል ናይ ምስራሕ ሓላፍነት ድማ ንማሕበራት ጥራሕ ዝምልከት ዘይኮነ፡ ንልቢ ኣብ ወጻኢ ናይ ዝርከቡ ብዙሓት ኤርትራውያን ክትንክፍ ዝኽኣለ ንከም በዓል ወዲ ቫካሮ ዝኣመሰሉ ውልቀ-ሰባት 'ውን ይምልከት እዩ። እዚ ክብል ዝደፍኣኒ ምኽንያት ድማ ካብ 'ቲ ኣብ ናይ ወዲ ቫካሮ ኣኼባታት ዝተራእየ ዋሕዚ ህዝብን ካብቲ ወዲ ቫካሮ ኣንጻር እቲ ኣብ ኣስመራ ዘሎ ስርዓት ንሓድነት ህዝቢ ዘርኣዮ ዘይሕለል ጻዕርታትን ተበጊሰ እየ። ኣብዚ ክንጥንቀቐሉ ዘሎና ነገር እንተሃልዩ፡ ካብ ሓድሐድ ምድግጋፍ ወጺእና፡ ኣብ መንጎ እዘን ዝቕልቀላ ዘለዋ ሓደስቲ ጉጅለታት ዘይተደልየ ምፍጣጥን ምጉርፋጥን ክይንፈጥር እዩ። ኩሎም ጉጅለታት የድልዩና

እዮም፡ ኩሎም ሰሚሮም ነቲ ጸቢብ ስረት ዘለዎ ውልቃዊ ወይ ጉጅልኣዊ ረብሓ ንጎኒ ገዲፎም፡ ነቲ ናይ ሓባር ዕላማ ኣብ ምዕዋት ሓቢሮም ክሰርሑ ከድሊ ‘ዩ። ሓንሳብ ነቲ እንምነዮ ዘሎና ናይ ስርዓት ለውጢ ምስ ጨበጥናዮ ድማ፡ ብኣማኢት ዝቖጸራ ናይ ሰነሓሳብ ጉጅለታት ይወዳደራ፡ ብዙሕነት ናይ ፖለቲካዊ ሰልፍታት ድማ ይዓምብብ።

ተወሰኽቲ ሕቶታት ንኹሎም ኤርትራውያን

1. ብዛዕባ እዞም ልዕል ኢሎም ኣብዚ ጽሑፍ ሰፊሮም ዘለዉ ኣሰቀቕቲ ተርእዮታት ናይ ኤርትራውያን እንታይ ሓሳባት ኣሎካ?
2. ኣብ ወጻኢ ዝርከቡ ኤርትራውያን እንታይ ክገብሩ ይግብኦም ትብል?
3. ናይ ኢሰይያስ ቀንዲ ድርኺት ምጅማር “ሃገራዊ ኣገልግሎት” ነቲ መንእሰይ ትውልዲ ኣብ ትሕቲ ምቁጽጽር ኣእትዩ ስልጣን ንምብሓት እዩ፡ ከም ‘ቲ ገለ ኤርትራውያን ዝብልዎ ህግደፍ ብዛዕባ ሳዋ ዘለዎ ፖሊሲ ክቅይር ‘ዩ ኢልካ ዶ ትግምት?
4. እቲ ዝበዝሐ ክፋል ኣብ ወጻኢ ዝነብር ኤርትራዊ ኣብ ደምበ ተቓውሞ ከይተጸንበረ ክተርፍ ምምራጹ በቲ ሓደ ሸንኽ፡ በቲ ካልእ ድማ እዚ ዘሎ ናይ ተቓውሞ ምንቅስቓሳት ነቲ ስርዓት ኣብ ምልዋጥ ይኹን፡ ንገዛእ ርእሱ ‘ውን ኣብ ፖሊሲኡ ይኹን ኣብ ‘ቲ ዝምርሓሉ ናይ ፖለቲካ መስመር ብቕዓት ከጥሪ ዘይምኽኣሉ፡ ሕጂ እንታይ ክግበር ኣለዎ ትብል?

ከጋጥሙ ዝኽእሉ ተርእዮታት

ብዓይኒ ሓቂ ጠሚትና እቲ ስርዓት ንናይ ህዝቢ ረብሓ ኣብ ዝውስነሉ እዋን ዊን ብዝበለ መንገድን ረብሓ ህዝቢ ዘየቖድምን ክሳብ ዝኾነ፡ ህዝቢ ኤርትራ ካብዞም ኣብ ታሕቲ ተጠቒሶም ዘለዉ ኣማራጺታት ሓደ ንከልዕል ተገዲዱ ኣሎ፡-

(ሀ) ከም ቀደሙ ክቕጽል?
(ለ) ስዕረቱ ተቐቢሉ ንህግደፍ ኣሜን ኢሉ ክምእዘዝን ኩሉ ናይ ምቅላስ መንፈሱ ደው ክብል?
(ሐ) ካልእ ናይ ቃልሲ ኣማራጺ መንገዲ ክናዲ?

ብዘይካ ደገፍቲ ህግደፍ ን(ሀ)ን (ለ) ከም ኣማራጺ መልስታት ዝወስድ ዋላ ሓደ ሰብ ኣሎ ኢለ ኣይግምትን። ስለዚ እቲ መልሲ (ሐ) እዩ ኢልካ ትሰማማዕ ዶ? እንተ ድኣ እቲ መልሲ እወ ኮይኑ፡ እንታይ ዓይነት ናይ ቃልሲ ሓድሽ ቅርጺ የድልየና፡ ምስ ‘ዘን ዝጸንሓ ውድባት ከ እንታይ ክንገብር ይግባእ?

ነዘን ኣብ ደምበ ተቓውሞ ዘለዋ ውድባት ንእለየን ኢልካ ምጥባቕ ኣገዳሲ ኣይኮነን ጥራሕ ዘይኮነ፡ ተግባራዊ ‘ውን ኣይኮነን። ተደላዪ ዘይኮነሉ ምኽንያት ድማ ናተን ታሪኽ ዘለወን፡ ብናይ ብዙሕ ህዝቢ ንዋትን ጻዕርን ብዙሕ ግዜ ጠፊእወን ብዙሓት ውፉያት ኣባላት ዝሓቖፉ፡ ድሉዋት ፖለቲካውን ሰብኣውን ዓቕሚ ዝሓዘላ ስለዝኾና። ካልእ ግብራዊ ዘይኮነሉ ምኽንያት ድማ፡ ንሰብ ከም ወዲ ሰብ መጠን ኣብ ግምት ኣእቲና፡ ነቲ ደቂ ሰባት ንነዊሕ እዋን ግዜኦምን ንዋቶምን ኣብ ‘ዘን ፖሊቲካውያን ሰልፍታትን ሲቪካውያን ማሕበራትን ኣጥፊኦም ዝኾነ ውጽኢት ከይረኣዩ ንኽገድፍወን ምእማን ዝከኣል ኣይኮነን። ብዝያዳ ‘ውን፡ ንኽገድፍወን ምድፋፋእ ኣሉታዊ ውጽኢት እዩ ክህልዎ ። ስለዚ እንታይ እዩ እቲ ክግበር ዝድለ ዘሎ?

መደምደምታ

ንድሕሪት ተመሊስ ክልተ ኣገደስቲ ጉዳያት ብምድህሳስ ክድምድም እየ። እታ ቀዳመይቲ ኣብ ኣድላይነት ቅዋም ምስምማዕ ክትከውን ከላ፡ እታ ካልኣይቲ ድማ ንጉዳይ ገበንን መቕጻዕትን እትምልከት እያ። ነቲ ቅዋም ብዝምልከት ዘለኒ ርእይቶ ዳርጋ ብሓፈሽኡ ፍሉጥ እዩ።

ከምቲ ወዲ ዓሊን ብጾቱን ዝኣመኑሉ፡ እቲ ናይ 1997 ቅዋም ንስርዓት ኢሳይያስ ካብ ስልጣን ንምእላይ ከም ናይ ሓባር መረዳድኢ ባይታ ከገልግል ይግባእ ዝብል ጽኑዕ እምነት ኣሎኒ። ድሕሪ ምውዳቕ ናይ ኢሳይያስ እቲ ዝምስረት ሃገራዊ ጉባኤ፡ እንተደልዩ ንገለ ክፋል ናይዚ ቅዋም ብምምሕያሽ ከጽድቖ ወይ’ውን ሓዲሽ ቅዋም ከጽድቕ ይኽእል። ነቲ ካልኣይ ጉዳይ ብዝምልከት፡ ገለ (ዳርጋ መብዛሕቶም) ኤርትራውያን ነዞም ናይ ሕጂ መራሕቲ መንግስቲ ኤርትራ ንናይ ቀደም ገበናቶም ኣመልኪቶም ክቕጽዑ ኣለዎም ክብሉ ከለዉ፡ ካልኦት ድማ ንረብሓ ሃገራዊ ሓድነትን ሰላምን ተባሂሉ ይቕረ ክግበረሎም ኣሎዎ ዝብል እምነት ዘለዎም ኣለዉ። እቶም ይቕረ ክግበረሎም ኣለዎ ዝብሉ ንሃገራዊ ዕርቂ ብምቕዳም ኣብ እዋን ብረታዊ ቃልሲ ዝተፈጸሙ ገበናት ዝሓለፈ ውሕጅ ይውሰዶ ተባሂሉ ክስገር ኣገዳሲ እዩ ይብሉ። እቶም ኣብ ግዜ ብረታዊ ቃልሲ ብናይ ተጋድሎ ሓርነትን ህዝባዊ ግንባርን መሪሕነት ግዳያት ዝኾኑ ኤርትራውያን ወይ ‘ውን ኣዝማድ ናይ ‘ቶም ግዳያት፡ ንሃገራዊ ዕርቂን ሓድነትን ተባሂሉ ይቕረ ክብሉ ንምእማን ከቢድ ስራሕ ክሓትት ይኸውን። ነዚ ጉዳይ ኣረዲእካ ከም ዝውሕጥዎ ምግባር ኣዝዩ መሪር ክኸውን ይኽእል፡ እንተኾነ ግን ብዛዕባ እቲ ካልእ ኣማራጺ ‘ውን ኣጸቢቕና ክንሓስብን ክነስተንትን ይግባኣና እዩ። ነቲ ዝዓበየ ረብሓ ክንጥምት ይግባኣና። ስፊሕ ሃገራዊ ክትዕ ከነካይድ ድማ ይግባእ። እዚ ምስ ገበንን መቕጻዕትን ዝተኣሳሰረ ጉዳይ ኣብ ክሊ ሞያይ እቱው ኮይኑ፡ ናይ ገለ ሃገራት ኣፍሪቃ ንደቡብ-ኣፍሪቃን ኡጋንዳን

ሰራልዮንን ላይበርያን ዝምልከት መጽናዕቲ ኣካይደ እየ። ኣብዚ ክልተ ዘይተርፉ ተጻረርቲ ዝመስሉ ግዴታት ኣለዉ። እቲ ሓደ ግዴታ ናይ ዕርቅን ሰላምን ክኸውን ከሎ፡ እቲ ካልኣይ ግዴታ ድማ ፍትሒ እዩ። ፍትሒ እቶም ገበነኛታት ናብ ፍርዲ ቀሪቦም ነቲ ዝፈጸምዎ ገበን ዝምልከት ግቡእ መቕጻዕቶም ክወስዱ ይጠልብ። እቶም ግዳያትን መቕርቦምን ድማ እቶም ገበነኛታት ናብ ፍርዲ ክቐርቡ ክጠልቡ ባህርያዊ እዩ። እዚ ድማ ባህርያዊን ትጽቢት ዝግበረሉን እዩ። በቲ ካልእ መዳይ ድማ፡ ከም ኣብ ገለ ሃገራት ኣፍሪቃ ዝተራእየ መወዳእታ ዘይብሉ ኲናት ወይ ‘ውን ከምዚ ናትና ዘይውዳእ ጭቆና ንምውጋድ፡ ማእከላይ ፍታሕ ንኽንቕበል እንግደደሉ ታሪኻዊ ኣጋጣሚ ክንወድቕ ንኽእል።

ኣብ ደቡብ-ኣፍሪቃ ናይ ሓቅን ዕርቅን ኮምሽን ብምቛም ገበነኛታት ናብቲ ኮምሽን ቀሪቦም ገበኖም ብምእማን ንስሓ ክገብሩን ይቕረታ ክሓቱን ዕድል ተዋሂብዎም እቶም ዝተናስሑ ይቕሬታ ተጌሩሎም። እቶም ናብቲ ኮምሽን ቀሪቦም ዘይተናስሑ ድማ ክሲ ቀሪብዎም ከም ዝቕጽዑ ተጌሩ።

ኣብዚ ዘለናዮ ኩነታት፡ እዞም ኣብ ደምበ ተቓውሞ እንርከብ ኤርትራውያን ነቲ ናይ ዶቡብ-ኣፍሪቃ ናይ ገበንን-መቕጻዕትን ኣገባብ ኣፈታትሓ ኣገባብ ክንቀድሖ ኣይንኽል ኢና። ቀዳማይ ነገር፡ ነቲ ነዚ ዕማም ዘሰላስል ኮሚሽን ክቐውም ዝኽእልን ነቲ መስርሕ ናይ ምክያድ ስልጣን ዝህብ መንግስትን ኣብ ቦትኡ ክህሉ ይግባእ። ንሕና ከምኡ ዓይነት መንግስቲ የብልናን፡ እንተኾነ ግን ኢሳይያስ፡ ንነብሱን ንካልኦት ኣብ ዝሓለፈ እዋን ገበን ፈጺሞም ተባሂሎም ዝጥርጠሩ ሰባትን ሓፈሻዊ ምሕረት ክዋሃቦም ምኳኑ ከም ዝኣምን ተጌሩ ነቲ ኮምሽን ሓቅን ዕርቅን ክቖሞ እንተተሰማሚዑ ግን እቲ ኮምሽን ክቐውም ይኽእል። ኣብዚ ኣብ ግምት ክኣቱ ዝግብኦ ግን፡ ብዙሓት ኣብ ተቓውሞ ዘለዉ ሰባት ነዚ ናይ ዝሓለፈ ገበናት ምሕረት ምሃብ ከይሰማምዕሉ ይኽእሉ ምኳኖም እዩ።

ኣብ መወዳእታ፡ ዜርና ዜርና እንወድቀሉ፡ ናይ ሕጂን ናይ ቀደምን ዕቑር ማሕበራዊ ሃብቲ ኣሎና። እዚ ናይ ዘበንና ማሕበራዊ ሃብቲ፡ ካብ ‘ዚ እነካይዶ ዘሎና ቃልሲ ተነጺሎምን ተገሊሎምን ዝጸንሑ ገጠምትን ሞያውያንን ዝሓቖፈ እዩ። እቲ ናይ ቀደም ማሕበራዊ ሃብትና ድማ፡ ገጠምትን ሞያውያንን ዝኾኑ ዓበይቲ ዓዲን መራሕቲ ሃይማኖትን ዘጠቓልል እዩ። ምብርባር ያታዊ ማሕበራዊ ሃብትና ኣብ ውሽጡ ክብርታት ኣለዎ፡ እቲ ናይ ምብርባር መስርሕ ንባዕሉ ‘ውን ክብሪ እዩ። ኣብ ‘ዚ ዘሎናዮ እዋን ክብርታትና ንምሕዳስን ምብርባርን ኣበርቲዕና ክንሰርሕ ይግባኣና፡ ብፍላይ ምስ ‘ቲ ናይ ጣዕሳን ምንጻህን ካሕሳን ዝብል መትከል ኣገናዚብና ክንሰርሕ ክንክእል መታን። ናይ ኤርትራ ዓበይቲ ዓድን ሽማግለታትን፣ ኣብ ወጻኢ ሃገር ናይ ዝርከቡ ናይ ሲቪል ይኹን ናይ ሃይማኖት መራሕቲ፣ ናይ ገጠምትን ሞያውያንን ኣስማት

እንስንደሉ ደብተር ከድልየና እዩ። እዚ ደብተር 'ዚ ዝርዝር ኣስማት ካብ ኣብ ደገ ዝርከባ ፖለቲካውያን ሰልፍታትን ሲቪካውያን ማሕበራትን 'ውን ዘጠቓልለ ክኸውን ይግባእ። እዞም ዝተጠቕሱ ሽማግለታት ዝፈልጥዎም ኣብ ውሽጢ ሃገር ዝርከቡ ሰባት ክህልዉ ግድን ስለ ዝኾነ ድማ፡ ነዚ ዕላማ ንምዕዋት ብዝጥዕሞም መንገዲ ብምስጢር ረኺቦም ክውድብዎምን ከስርሕዎምን ምግባር ከድሊ ዩ።

እዞም ኣቕሪበዮም ዘለኹ ርእይቶታትን መፍትሒታትን ምስ ዘለናዮ ተሃዋሲ ኩነታት ሃገርና ኣብ ሓደጋ ንከይትወድቕ ኣቓልቦ ተዋሂብዎም ብህጹጽ ክፍትሑ ኣለዎም ኢለ ዝኣመንኩሎም ነጥብታት 'የም። ሃገርና ካብ 'ዚ ኣጋጢምዋ ዘሎ ሓደጋ፡ ከነድሕና ኣሎና ንብል እንተ ኼና ድማ ነዞም ነጥብታት ኣብ ግምት ከነእትዎም ኣሎና ዝብል ዘይንቕነቕ እምነት ኣሎኒ። እቲ ዝግባእ ኣቓልቦ ድማ ኣብ 'ዚ ከይተሓጽረ ኪኖ 'ዚ ዓውደ-መጽናዕቲ ዝጠመተ ክኸውን ይግባእ እብል። መንቀሊ ናይ 'ዚ ሕጂ ዝጽውዖ ዘለኹ ቅልጡፍ ፍታሕ፡ እቲ ግዜ ዘይህብ ሓደገኛ ኩነታት ሃገርና ዘንቀሎ ጥራሕ ዘይኮይነ፡ እታ ኣብ ሓደ እዋን ተስፋ ዝተነብረላ ሃገርና ንዘልኣለም ንከይትጠፍእን ንከይንስእናን ካብ ዘለኒ ስግኣት ዝብገስ እዩ። እዚ ህጽጽ ጻውዒት ድማ ብዝያዳ ነዞም ናይ 'ዚ ሓድሽ ሚለንዩም ትውልድን ነቶም ካብኣቶም ብዕድመ ብርኽ ዝበሉን፡ ሃገርና ካብ ናይ ብረታዊ ቃልሲ ሃፈጽታ ክትገላገል ከላ ዕድሚኦም ኣብ ዓሰርተታት ዝነበሩ መንእሰያት ዘተኮረ እዩ። ንስኹምን፡ ንሕና እዞም ዝሸምገልና ማይና ዝሰተናን፡ ሃገር ክትበታተንን ክትጠፍእን እንዳ ረኣና ኣዒንትና ዓሚትና ስቕ ኢልና ተዓዚብቲ ኴና ዲና ክንተርፍ ወይስ ዋልታ ሃገር ኴና ሃገርና ከነድሕን ዝብል ሕቶ ድማ ክንምልሶ ይግባእ!!

እዚ ወዳሓንኩም!!!

041114-300-1-60W

صالح يونس

ورقة دكتور برخت هبتى سلاسي ، (في مسارنا للتغيير) تذكر المرء واحدة من أقوال لينين المشهورة (ما الذي يجب عمله) وهو سؤال الساعة في حراكنا الجاري ، ليس هذا وحسب بل واحد من العناوين الجانبية للورقة يحمل ذات التعبير (ما الذي يجب عمله) الورقة تحمل البعدين التشخيصي وتوصيف العلاج . على عكس لينين الذي دخل في جدل نخبوي مع العلماء والمنظرين في عصره فإن دكتور برخت ظل يقود لوحدة حملة ضد النظام طوال العقد الماضي متجاوزاً بذلك حالة الانفصام عن القضية لدى معظم الاكاديمين الإرتريين وغيابهم عن التعاطي مع القضايا الساخنة في الوقت الحاضر ، أنها نقطة تحسب لصالح دكتور برخت وهو يتقدم بمشروع قابل للتنفيذ يدعو الجميع من خلاله لتجاوز حالة المراقبة ليكونوا ضمن موجة التغيير المرتجي.

في توصيف دكتور برخت فإن المشكلة الحقيقة في إرتريا تكمن في أن اسياس وحزبه تمكنوا من الهيمنة الكاملة على كافة مفاصل الوطن وكافة سلطاته التنفيذية والتشريعية والقضائية ، واصبحت تلك السلطات المطلقة وسيلتهم لتنفيذ سياسات مضرة وخاطئة ، حتى اصبحت ارتريا معلقة بين البقاء والانهيار.

يعود دكتور برخت الى السؤال الجوهري ، ما الذي يجب عمله؟ ويري أن هنالك خيارات ثلاثة امام قوى التغيير ، وهي ، الاستمرار والمواصلة في العمل على الوتيرة الحالية ، أو الاعتراف بالهزيمة والاستسلام للظلم ، او إيجاد خيار آخر لتسريع نضالنا لتحقيق التغيير المنشود. وبما أن الخيار الأخير هو الخيار المقبول عليه فإن دكتور برخت يقترح بديل جديد وهو انشاء جبهة متحدة (ليست بالضرورة وحدة كاملة او اندماجية) مع التأكيد أن هذه الجبهة ليست ملزمة لأى أحد من أعضائها بعد انجاز الهدف الاساسي وهو اسقاط النظام.

إن هذا الخيار باعتراف دكتور برخت قد جرت عدة محاولات لإنجازه ، وتفصل الورقة كافة المعيقات التي حالت دون تحقيقه على الوجه المطلوب منها : هل تكون وسائلنا للتغيير سلمية ام عسكرية ، طبيعة علاقتنا باثيوبيا ؟ دور منظمات المجتمع المدني والتنيظمات السياسية ، هل نحن نبحث عن العدالة ام السلام والمصالحة؟ هل الارتريون في الخارج يقودون التغيير ام يكونوا أداة داعمة ومشجعة للقوى في الداخل ؟ هل نستخدم دستور 1997م ام نركز في البحث عن الدولة الدستورية . إن دكتور برخت لا يقترح خارطة طريق للتغيير بقدر سعيه الى بلورة الخيارات المتاحة لتحفيز الساحة لنقاش حقيقي بالتركيز على خيار الجبهة المتحدة التي يعتبرها ذات أهمية قصوى ، دكتور برخت يدعو وكما لينين في السابق الى تجاوز حالة الانقسام والتفكك والتردد ومواجهة المخاطر التي تهدد بقاء إرتريا.

في مسارنا للتغيير الديمقراطي ، قضايا يجب إنجازها ومزالق يلزم تفاديها

برخت هبتي سيلاسي
بروفيسور في القضايا الدراسات الافريقية والقانون
جامعة نورث كارولينا - كابيتل هيل
ورقة مقدمة في ورشة العمل التي نظمتها الحركة الارترية للديمقراطية وحقوق الانسان
بريتوريا - 09-2014/05/11م

في البدء سوف استعرض محتويات الورقة ، والتي تتكون من خمسة أجزاء بما فيه المقدمة التي تشكل الجزء الأول من الورقة ، الفصل الثاني وهو توصف للمأزق الذي نعيشه من خلال تحليل سياسي واقتصادي واجتماعي للمشكلات ، في الجزء الثالث اشرت الى قضايا لا بد من إنجازها حتى نتمكن من تجاوز المشكلات التي اشرت اليها في الفصل السابق ، الجزء الرابع يستشرف المستقبل ويطرح اسئلة حرجة ، ويقترح بعض الحلول المبدئية لتلك الاسئلة ، الجزء الخامس يحتوى على خلاصة الورقة ، وقد حاولت إثارة

القضايا الجدلية من منظور أوسع من خلال المفهوم التاريخي ، وقد أثرت أيضاً قضية الدستور والدور الذي يمكن أن يلعبه في الاسهام في حل المشكلات العالقة .

في الوقت الذي بدأت العديد من الاراء والمقترحات بدأت تتداعي لضرورة وحدة الجهود في معركة اسقاط النظام الدكتاتوري في اسمرا ، وفي سبيل ذلك الهدف رأيت من المناسب ان أطرح ورقة يمكن أن تسهم في تشكيل الإطار العام للنقاش ، ولهذا الهدف جاءت هذه الورقة.

المقدمة :-

مما لاشك ان تقييم مختصر للحالة التي تعيشها إرتريا ، والعناصر الرئيسية في تشكيل هذه الحالة ضروري جداً كخلفية لرسم إطار للقضايا المصيرية التي تواجهنا كشعب ، خاصة في المرحلة الانتقالية حيث يتطلب رسم خارطة طريق للمرحلة التي تلي زوال النظام الحالي.

إن العديد من المثقفين والناشطين عقدوا العديد من الاجتماعات ، وإداروا حوارات تتركز حول كيفية مواجهة المأزق الذي يعيشه شعبنا ، كما إنه في الآوانة الأخيرة شهدنا العديد من المبادرات تطالب بالتوافق الوطني حول الاهداف الاساسية من أجل توحيد الجهود ، إن التماثل في الافكار والمشاعر في كافة تلك المساعي والمبادرات أمر مذهل وطبيعي ، لأن الجميع يسعي الى تجميع وتنسيق الجهود من أجل الحفاظ على الوقت والموارد ، ولتفادي التكرار والازدواجية .

إن هدفي من طرح الورقة هو تقديم مساهمة متواضعة في تحقيق رؤية واضحة ومتجانسة لتحقيق وحدة الجهود من أجل الاهداف المشتركة ، وفي سبيل ذلك الهدف فقد اعتمدت الورقة في معظم جوانبها المنهج السقراطي بإتباع طرح الاسئلة بدلا عن اصدار احكام ، ما عدا فيما يتعلق بالدستور ودوره كإطار لتأمين وضمان الاعتراف المتبادل كأساس للتعايش الوطني ، حيث عمدت الورقة الى طرح حلول ومقترحات للمشكلات ، وقد جاء إثارة بعض القضايا الجدلية في بعض جوانب الورقة مقصوداً في ذاته لإثارة النقاش مثل كيفية التعاطي مع الجرائم التي ارتكبت اثناء فترة النضال المسلح لتحرير الوطن.

ربما قد يتساءل البعض وهم محقين عن جدوى محاضرة تقدم عن طريق فرد في ظل الظروف المأساوية التي يعيشها شعبنا ، منطلقين من ايمانهم أن المطلوب هو حوار ممتد بين الارتريين ، ومع ذلك ربما محاضرة كهذه يمكن ان تساهم في الحوار الوطني حول ماهية المطلوب لتحقيق توافق وطني لإيجاد حلول مستدامة ، كلكم تابعتم في الآونة الاخيرة المحاضرات التي قدمت بواسطة فرد واحد مصمم ومتفاني وهو تولدي تسفاماريام (ودي فاكارو) قد اوضحت جلياً إن الحديث الصادق النابع من القلب حتى إن كان من شخص واحد يمكن ان يكون لها اثر كبير على المجتمع بشكل اوسع. الآن بعض المحاضرات العديدة التي قدمها تولدي البعض بدأ يتساءل ، ثم ماذا بعد ؟ الى أين سيقودنا هذا فيما يتعلق بعمل جدّي على الأرض ، هذه أسئلة جيدة ، وهو ما جعلنى اقدم ورقتي هذه كمحاولة للاجابة على سؤال ، ما الذي يجب فعله على أرض الواقع لإحداث التغيير المنشود.

إن موضوع ورشة بريتوريا يغطي العديد من القضايا التي تعني المشكلات الارترية ، ولسهولة العرض اقترح جمع الموضوعات بشكل عام تحت العناوين السياسية ، الاقتصادية ، الاجتماعية ، وعليه سوف اواصل على هذا المنوال مبتدئاً بسرد للعناصر الاساسية للمحنة الارترية من خلال منظور تاريخي . إن النقاش وسط الارتريين حول القضايا خاصة المتعلقة بموضوع تاريخ النضال الارتري تنطوي غالبا على منظور تنافسي وهي تعكس بشكل او آخر وجهة نظر التنظيمين المتنافسين تاريخياً (جبهة التحرير الإرترية ، والجبهة الشعبية لتحرير إرتريا) ولكن في الآونة الأخيرة ظهرت بعض المحاولات التوفيقية الشجاعة بين السرديين المتنافسين . حتماً انه في ظل العمل لصالح هدف واحد ومواجهة عدو مشترك فإن مثل هذه المحاولات تعتبر مبشرة ومشجعة.

الوضع الراهن وأهم عناصره :-

إنه من المحزن جداً بعد عشرين عاماً من استقلال ارتريا وخروج المستعمر الاثيوبي أن تكون بلادنا على مفترق طرق ، تقف متأرجحة بين البقاء والانهيار ، إن مأساة لامبيدوزا تعتبر لحظة تاريخية تجعلنا أمام الحقيقة المرة ، الحقيقة التي لا جدال فيها هي أن شباب إرتريا ركيزة وضمان المستقبل يعيش على حافة فقدان الأمل في المستقبل ، ووطن من غير شباب من غير آمال او طموحات هو وطن لا مستقبل له ، إن الحكومة الارترية التي بدأت مبشرة بالديمقراطية ، الرخاء ، وحكم القانون ، أصبحت للاسف السبب في نزاعات لا نهاية لها ، والمحصلة لذلك هو معاناة ويأس يكتنف شعبها ، إن حكومة اسياس أفورقي وحزبه - الجبهة الشعبية للديمقراطية

والعدالة - لم يجلبوا للشعب لا الديمقراطية ولا العدالة ، بالتأكيد فهم قد حنثوا بوعدهم ، واهدروا الموارد وأضاعوا فرصاً ذهبية ، مفضلين الانخراط في سياسات تخريبية خطيرة ، إن تبنى النظام ما عرف بالخدمة الوطنية وهو في الحقيقة عبودية قسرية دفع جيل كامل من الشباب الارتري للضياع ، حارماً الاباء من دعم ومساندة ابنائهم في سنوات عمرهم الذهبية ، إن هروبهم من وضع كهذا هو ما دفع بهم الى الغرق في لامبيدوزا ، وحوادث غرق مماثلة سابقة في البحر الابيض المتوسط وإن كانت باعداد أقل. دعني الخّص الواقع المرير لحال الكثير من الارتريين كما صورتها مآساة لامبيدوزا:-

- هنالك انتهاكات مستمرة للحقوق الاساسية للانسان ، تلك الحقوق التي ضمنها الدستور المصادق عليه في عام 1997م ، وكذلك في كافة القوانين والاعراف الدولية.

- إن البلاد تحكم من خلال توجيهات صادرة من مكتب رئيس غير منتخب ، مثل هذه التوجيهات لا تخضع لأي مراجعة وتعتبر تجاوز لكل مفاهيم سيادة القانون.

- الحزب الحاكم - الجبهة الشعبية للديمقراطية والعدالة - يحتكر عملياً كافة النشاط الاقتصادي في البلاد من خلال المكتب الاقتصادي العملاق - شركة البحر الاحمر والشركات التابعة لها.

- عسكرة المجتمع تعتبر علمياً أعتقال وحشي لكافة مكونات المجتمع ، حيث يخضع كافة الذكور في الاعمار بين 18 - 50 سنة ، والاناث بين 18-40 سنة للخدمة العسكرية مفتوحة الأجل.

- نتيجة لهذه السياسات والممارسات حدث تفكك اجتماعي واقتصادي ، بما في ذلك تعطيل العملية التعلمية والمعيشية لجيل كامل.

- وقبل كل ذلك فإنه تم النكوث عن الوعد بالانتقال الديمقراطي نحو حكومة دستورية لصالح حكم الحزب الواحد - ثم الرجل الواحد ، كل هذا في انتهاك كامل لكافة قرارات مؤتمرات الجبهة الشعبية ، وأحكام دستور عام 1997م ، وعليه يمكن القول إن هذا الانتهاك هو السبب الرئيس لكافة الأزمات في إرتريا.

عناصر الأزمة:-

سياسات الهيمنة والإقصاء:-

كما سبق توضيحه ، فإن الحكومة مبنية على احتكار السلطة بواسطة حزب يقوده رئيسه اسياس افورقي ، وبالرغم من وجود مسميات للسلطات التي تتكون منها الحكومات ، التشريعية والتنفيدية والقضائية ، ولكن الحقيقة هي إن الجهاز التنفيذي الذي يقوده اسياس افورقي هو الذي يهيمن ويحتكر كافة السلطات في سخرية واضحة من مفهوم القانون وفصل السلطات ، إن كافة السلطات تمت مركزتها في إطار ضيق يتحكم فيه رجل واحد يساعده مجموعة من العصابة من مرتزقة الحزب، وهو ما ينطبق على الإدارات الاقليمية حيت تم توزيع ارتريا الى ستة أقاليم تدار اسمياً من خلال حاكم يتم تعينه من قبل الرئيس ، ولكن منذ عام 2000م ، اصبح لزاماً على حاكم الاقليم بقرار من الرئيس رفع تقاريره الى قيادة المنطقة العسكرية التي تقع

في الاقليم - عادة هذه المناطق العسكرية تقاد من خلال الجنرالات - والجنرالات بدورهم يرفعون تقاريرهم للرئيس ، هذا الوضع عزز عسكرة الحكومة والمجتمع وعمق الاحساس والشعور بالعجز لدى المجتمع المدني الذي تم ترهيبه لالتزام الصمت .

يمكن القول بعبارة واحدة إن المشكلة الاساسية في ارتريا اليوم هي الغياب الكامل لمبدأ المحاسبة والشفافية ، ولهذا فإن الرئيس الغير مسئول بدء الحرب على اثيوبيا في عام 1998م ، من غير استشارة الحكومة او الجمعية الوطنية ، وبلغت الأمور ذروتها عقب الحرب الكارثية عندما تحدى اعضاء بارزين في الجبهة الشعبية والحكومة ، الرئيس مطالبين بمساءلته ، ولهذا الغرض فإنهم طالبوا باجتماع القيادة المركزية للحزب وكذلك الجمعية الوطنية باعتبارها الجهاز التشريعي للدولة ، على أن يقوم الاجتماع بإعادة تقييم القرار الذي دفع البلاد الى الحرب وهو ما ترتب عليه احتلال جزء مقدر من التراب الارتري بواسطة القوات الاثيوبية. بمعنى أن مجموعة كانوا من رفقاء الرئيس في حرب التحرير ، وزملاء في الحكومة التي كان ولايزال يهيمن عليها لسنوات وهم المجموعة التي عرفت بمجموعة الخمسة عشر **(G15)** تحدوا اسياس للمرة الأولي ، وفكروا في اخضاعه للمحاسبة لبدءه الحرب دون مشاورتهم او استشاره الجمعية الوطينة ، وكان رده متعجرفاً جداً برفض الاجتماع ، مصحوباً بتهديدات من قبيل ان ما يقومون به ستكون له عواقب وخيمة اذا لم يرعوى عن مطالبهم.

في اعقاب الهجوم الارهابي على الولايات المتحدة في الحادي عشر من سبتمبر 2001م ، مستقلاً انشغال العالم بالحدث ، أصدر اسياس أوامره باعتقال 11 شخص من المجموعة ، وكذلك محرري

ومراسلي الصحافة الحرة التي تم تأسيسها حديثاً ودرجت على كتابة ونشر مقالات تنتقد الحكومة ، وإجراء مقابلات مع بعض اعضاء مجموعة الـ **(G15)** ، إن هذه الاعتقالات للقيادات والصحفيين شغلت الرأى العام الارتري خاصة الجاليات في الخارج. وقد أدى ذلك الى بروز احزاب جديدة تعارض النظام ، ومنظمات مجتمع مدني تطالب بالرقابة والمحاسبة على اعمال الحكومة فيما يتعلق بحقوق الانسان وتنفيذ دستور عام 1997م. على عكس الآمال وتوقعات الكثير من المفكرين الارتريين ، فإن ما قام به اسياس في مقابل المطالب التي تقدم بها مجموعة الـ **(G15)** وغيرهم من افراد الشعب الارتري فاق كل التوقعات ، الرئيس فعلا دعا لاجتماع الجمعية الوطنية ولكن ليس تحقيقاً لمطلب مجموعة الـ **(G15)** ، ولكن لتقديم اقتراح بإتهام مجموعة الـ **(G15)** بالخيانة وغيرها من الجرائم ، للاسف فإن الجمعية في طاعة عمياء للرئيس قبلت الاقتراح ، وفي يوم 18 سبتمبر 2001م فإن 11 من مجموعة الـ **(G15)** تم اعتقالهم بمعزل عن العالم الخارجي في مكان غير معروف (صادف ان 3 من اعضاء المجموعة كانوا متواجدين في الخارج واصبحوا لاحقاً جزء من حركة معارضة النظام).

كما رأينا فإنه لدينا جميعة وطنية مطيعة لمطالب الرئيس ، ولكن ماذا عن السلطة القضائية؟ بداية واعدة جداً لبدء عمل مؤسسي مع المصادقة على دستور 1997م الذي ضمن استقلالية القضاء ، رئيس المحكمة العليا سعى حثيثاً لأعطاء القوة الكافية التي تضمن عمل السلطة القضائية بشكل مستقل عن السلطة التنفيذية ، وخلال مؤتمر دولي عقد في اسمرا ، تحدث رئيس القضاء عن تدخل السلطة التنفيذية في سلطة القضاء وقد انتقد علناً الرئيس ، وشهادة للتاريخ فإن احداً من الحاضرين في المؤتمر لم ينطق بكلمة دعم او مساندة ،

أو طرح سؤالاً او تعليقاً حول كلمة رئيس القضاء ، من الواضح فإن الصمت الناجم عن التخويف لم يتوقف تأثيره على الإرتريين ولكن حتى الأجانب من أصدقاء ارتريا الذين حضروالمؤتمر ، ولم تمضي ايام على الحادثة حتى تم الاستغناء عن رئيس القضاء بواسطة الرئيس. غني عن القول فإن الرئيس الذي يقود الدولة ، ويتولي قيادة القوات المسلحة ، وعليه فمن الطبيعي أن يسيطر على كافة القوى العسكرية والأمنية ، وبالتالي يترأس مجتمع عسكري ، بإختصار إنه دكتاتور كلمته بمثابة القانون.

اقتصاد الدولة ، الاحتكار والحرمان :-

إن إقتصاد إرتريا اليوم في حالة من الفوضى الشاملة ، شعار الاعتماد على الذات الذي كان مفيداً في مرحلة الكفاح المسلح ، لم تتوقف فائدة على تلك المرحلة وحسب ، ولكن اصبح حلة دائمة لا يستطيع الاقتصاد الارتري عنها فكاكاً ، علاوة على ذلك فإن الاقتصاد الموجه الذي ورثته إرتريا من الحكومة الاثيوبية إبان عهد الدرق لم يتم التخلي عنه بواسطة النظام ، وهو الاقتصاد الذي يعتمد في مبادئه على الايدلوجية الماركسية اللينينة ، المشروعات الخاصة التي كانت واعدة في ظل الاقتصاد المختلط لم يتم تشجيعها ، والأدهي من ذلك إن الحكومة رفعت شعار النموذج السنغافوري ولكن كل مشاريع التنمية فشلت ، إن الظروف التي أوصلت الاقتصاد في سنغافورة الى مصاف الاقتصاديات المتقدمة لا تنطبق على الاقتصاد الإرتري - الزراعة - الثروة الحيوانية - الصناعات الخفيفة - لا يمكن أن توفر قاعدة ثابتة لإنطلاق اقتصاد على غرار نموذج سنغافوره ، إن الأمال المعقودة على الثروة البحرية ، المعادن ، والسياحة والتي

كان يتوقع لها أن تلفت نظر الاستثمارات الاجنبية وتوفر سوق عمالة محلية تحطمت على صخرة السياسات الخاطئة ، والممارسات الكارثية ، والمحصلة انها لم تستطع أن تجذب الاستثمارات المتوقعة.

أعلنت الحكومة إن أولوياتها هي تنمية الموارد البشرية ، ربما لأنها تاثرت بالنموذج السنغافوري ، ولتحقيق هذا الهدف عملت على إعادة صياغة السياسات الإدارية ويبدو انه كان لديها آمال كبيرة ، ولكن هذه الاهداف تمت هزيمتها من خلال عسكرة المجتمع ، وتخصيص نصيب الأسد في الميزانية لقطاع الأمن ، وحرمان قطاعات التعليم والقطاعات الاجتماعية ، علاوة على ذلك فإنه لم يجري نقاش موضوعي عام حول السياسات المناسبة للتعليم بما فيه قطاع التعليم العالي ، الجامعة الوحيدة في البلاد تم اضعافها بشكل مطرد ، وتم اغلاقها في نهاية المطاف لمصلحة الكليات التقنية التي تم تدشينها في مناطق قليلة ويرأسها قيادات عسكرية ، طلاب هذه الكليات المزدوجة ملزمون بالخدمة العسكرية حيث يعتبرون قوات احتياط ، ويمكن استدعائهم لإداءها في أى وقت ، تعتبر الحكومة مشروع العمالة الغير مدفوعة الأجر أقصر الطرق الى تحقيق التنمية الاقتصادية ، ولكن النتائج لم تؤكد الأهداف المطلوبة ، بالمقابل فإنه ثبت انها إهدار للموارد البشرية ، وتسببت في معاناة الشعب ، والتفكك الاجتماعي كما سبق توضيحه.

الخلاصة ، استناداً الى أداء الاقتصاد خلال الاعوام الماضية فإن المؤكد إن المستقبل قاتم والتوقعات غير مبشرة ، إن معدل النمو المحلي يتوقع ان يبقى تحت الـ 2% ، حتى مع عائدات قطاع التعدين. إن مصادر النمو الرئيسية مثل المشروعات الممولة من الخارج ، او تحويلات الارتريين في الشتات وهو ما يجعل الحكومة تسعى

بإصرار لفرض ضريبة الـ 2% على كل الارتريين في الخارج كشرط لتقديم الخدمات الاجتماعية والانسانية مثل اعطاء التصاريح لممارسة النشاطات الاجتماعية مثل الزواج ، ومراسيم الدفن عند الوفيات وغيرها من الخدمات التي يتوقعها المواطن من أى حكومة شرعية ، إن آثار اقتصاد الحرمان الذي يتباه النظام ظهرت جلياً في حياة المواطنين .

الوضع الاجتماعي المتدهور:-

من الطبيعي أن يتأثر الوضع الاجتماعي في كل بلد بتدهور الاقتصاد والأزمات السياسية ، وهو الحال الماثل في إرتريا منذ اكثر من عقد من الزمان ، وقد ازداد الأمر سوءاً بعد الحرب الارترية الاثيوبية في الفترة من 1998-2000م ، ولكن قبل هذه الحرب المدمرة فإن ممارسة سياسة الهيمنة والاقصاء بواسطة الجبهة الشعبية للديمقراطية والعدالة التي أقصت كافة الاحزاب والتنظيمات السياسية الأخرى ، إضافة الى الاحتكار الكامل للاقتصاد بواسطة الحكومة كان مؤشراً واضحاً الى هذا المآل المتمثل في الأزمة الاجتماعية . واذا نظرنا الى الوضع الاجتماعي قياساً على مؤشر الامم للتنمية البشرية عام 2004م الصادر عن برنامج الامم المتحدة الانمائي (**UNDP**) ، فإن إرتريا ضمن الدول التي تكاد تتذيل القائمة وجاء ترتيبها في المرتبة 157 من بين 177 دولة ، راجع (**UNDP HDI Report, 2006**).

إن مؤشر التنمية البشرية السابق ذكره مفيد جدا في قياس رفاهية الانسان متجاوزاً معايير معدل التنمية المحلي (**GDP**) لانه يستصحب عدة أبعاد للتنمية البشرية مثل توفر الغذاء وامكانية الحصول عليه باسعار معقولة ، توفر التعليم وسهولة الحصول عليه

مادياً ، يسر الخدمات الصحية الجيّدة ، توفر السكن في مناطق آمنة باسعار مقدور عليها ، وقياساً على هذا المؤشر الذي يستصحب الابعاد المذكورة فإن إرتريا سجلت مرتبة متدنية للغاية في استطلاع تم إجراءه في عام 2006م ، وهو الاستطلاع الذي أظهر بما لا يدع مجالاً للشك فشل ارتريا في توفير الخدمات الاساسية المذكورة إنه مؤسفاً جدا أن يتحول شعب فخور وكادح ، الى شعب متسول يعتمد على سخاء المانحين من الخارج في بقاءه او توفير الامور الاساسية مثل الغذاء ، صحيح أن موجة الجفاف لها تأثيرها في الحاضر كما كان في الماضي ، ولكن لا يمكن بأى حال من الأحوال القاء اللوم على الطبيعة فيما يتعلق بمعاناة الشعب الارتري . إن السياسات والممارسات الخاطئة هي المسؤول الحقيقي عن هذه المعاناة ، إنه لمن المفارقات أن حكومة تعلن اشمئزازها ليل نهار من المساعدات الخارجية أصبحت عملياً تعتمد عليها بشكل مطرد ، بالرغم من رفضها أن تلعب المنظمات الدولية الغير حكومية دوراً في توفير الاحتياجات الاساسية للسكان.

إن أحد الابعاد المأساوية للازمة الاجتماعية في إرتريا اليوم تتعلق بالمسنين ، الذين تركوا ليتدبروا أمورهم بأنفسهم ، في الوقت الذي كان يفترض ان يتم الاعتناء بهم بواسطة ابنائهم ، وكان يمكن أن يحدث ذلك ، ولكن هؤلاء الابناء الآن هم بالألاف موزعين بين الخنادق جنوداً ضمن برنامج ما عرف بالخدمة الوطنية ، التي تستهلك اعمارهم في وقت كان يجب ان يكونوا في مقاعد التعليم او يربون ابنائهم ، تاركين ابائهم يعانون الوحدة والاهمال في هذا العمر المتقدم ، كما أن الآلاف منهم فروا الى الدول المجاورة ، والى ما هو ابعد من ذلك ، وحادثة لامبيدوزا خير شاهد على ذلك ، أما الذين لم تتاح لهم فرصة الهروب فهم يعيشون حياة اشبه بالسجن والعبودية.

قد تجد السلع المستوردة مكتظة في رفوف المحلات التجارية ، ولكن بالمقابل فإن الصفوف الطويلة للحصول على الخبز أصبحت منظراً مألوفاً ، يبدأ الاصطفاف في هذه الصفوف من الخامسة صباحاً ، وينتظرون الساعات الطوال حتى يأتي من يخبرهم بأن الخبز قد انتهى ولا يوجد المزيد منه وعليكم القدوم يوم غد ، المدارس المزدحمة لا تتوفر لها كتب ومعدات تعليمية كافية ، والمعلمون يتاقضون رواتب لا تكفى الى نهاية الشهر ، الخدمات الصحية متدهورة للغاية والمحظوظين هو القلة التي تتاح لها فرصة الحصول على العلاج في الخارج ، هذا حال شعب كان يفاخر بالخدمات الصحية المتطورة في المناطق المحررة إبان مرحلة الكفاح المسلح.

على ضوء هذه الواقع المؤسف يحق للمرء ان يتساءل كيف إن الوطنيين منذ ذوي التفكير السليم استطاعوا التعايش مع هذه الحكومة في مثل هذه الظروف ، والإجابة هي انهم يفعلون ما بوسعهم لمواجهة التحدي المتمثل في التدهور المستمر لحال الشعب الإرتري ، ولكن جهودهم لم تكن على قدر المطلوب ببساطة لأنهم يعملون في ظروف محكومة بسياسات وممارسة سيئة لا يمكلون السيطرة عليها ، إن كافة المحاولات للتشكيك في السياسات او توجيه انتقادات للنظام ترتبت عليها نتائج وخيمة ، إن اعتقال **(G15)** والصحفيين يعتبر بمثابة تحذير ، مصحوباً بالتوسع في تشديد الرقابة الامنية على كافة الكلمات والافعال ، إن الاجهزة الامنية تراقب الجميع وفي كافة الاوقات ، وعليه لا شئ يمكن عمله من الداخل ، لهذا فإن كافة الانظار معلقة بالإرتريين في الخارج الذين تزايدت أعدادهم الى عشرة اضعاف في العقد الأخير.

ما الذي يجب فعله:-

في سياق الازمات السياسية ، الاقتصاية ، والاجتماعية التي تم توصفيها ، السؤال الذي يلح على ذهن أى إرتري اليوم هو ما الذي يحب فعله : اولاً لتغيير الوضع المأساوي ، وثانياً لتلافي تكرار اخطاء الماضي مرة اخرى؟

إن أى محاولة للاجابة على هذا السؤال تبدأ من الحاجة الماسة للوحدة الوطنية . في الحادي عشر من يناير 2009م ، كنت مدعواً الى تقديم كلمة في المؤتمر التأسيسي لمنظمة - إرتريون من أجل الحقوق الديمقراطية في إرتريا - سدري - الذي عقد في لندن بالمملكة المتحدة ، وفي تلك المناسبة هنأت اللجنة المنظمة للمؤتمر على المبادرة ، وقلت لهم إنني أعتبر تأسيس منظمتهم واحدة من العلامات البارزة في النضال الإرتري من أجل النهوض بالقيم الديقراطية وسيادة القانون في بلادنا المظلمة لجهة إنعدام هذه القيم .

وهنا تجدر الاشارة الى ظهور عدد من المنظمات المدنية ذات الاهداف المماثلة لسدري ، ويعتبر هذا اتجاه مشجع ، ويعطي الأمل للمجتمع الإرتري في الخارج الذي كاد ان يعتريه اليأس.

عنواني خطابي في مؤتمر سدري كان (الوحدة الوطينة من أجل المصلحة العامة : تأملات مسن في مأزق شعبه) لقد خاطبت الحضور مذكراً إن ورقتي تعكس طريقة تفكير رجل ينتقل الى مرحلة يقل فيها النشاط ، ويغلب عليها التأمل سواء في حياته العلمية أو العملية ، وقد جاءت عباراتي مفاجأة لبعض الحضور الذين ربما اعتقدوا انني لا اتأثر بعامل العمر ، خاصة عندما ذكرت انه اثناء مرحلة السبعين من العمر أود أن أوكد انني مدرك تماماً لضرورة

الاستعجال وأهمية الوقت لجهة أن هنالك مهمة لم تكتمل بعد ، والتي أتمنى مخلصاً ان تكتمل ، وسوف اخصص جزء كبيراً مما تبقى مع العمر للمساعدة في اكمالها ، واحدة من المهمام الكبيرة التي لم تكتمل وتحتاج الى جهود هي الانقسامات المستمرة بين الارتريين في الوقت الذي تعيش فيه البلاد تحت قبضة دكتاتور لا يرحم ، وقد وضع البلاد على حافة الانهيار.

خمسة سنوات مرت على ذلك الخطاب ونحن لا نزال مقسمين اكثر من أي وقت مضى ، واحد من الاسئلة الاساسية التي لا تزال محل خلاف مستمر ، هو كيف يمكن حل مشكلة شعبنا ، كيف نحدث التغيير ، وكيف ننقذ شعبنا الذي عاني طويلا ولايزال من قبضة براثن النظام الاستبدادي . إنه أمر يستحق التذكير إن استمرا ر الازمة الحالية لوطننا دون حل يمكن ان يترتب عليها نتائج كارثية وتكون نهاية وطن بمعنى الكلمة ، هذه الاحتمالية يجب ان تساعدنا في التركيز للوصول الى حلول في الوقت المناسب. إن المطلب الأول الذي يجب أن نركز عليه هو ايجاد جبهة موحدة تسعى لتغيير النظام ، والتبشير بنظام ديمقراطي ، الكثيرمن الارتريين في الخارج بذلوا جهوداً مقدرة تهدف الى إيجاد او المساهمة في إيجاد جبهة موحدة ، الجميع يبدو مقتنعا من حيث المبدأ بضرورة إيجاد جبهة موحدة ، وانه يجب أن لا نبقى مقسمين في الوقت الذي يعاني فيه شعبنا من قبضة الدكتاتور وعصابته التي تسعى الى تدمير بلادنا.

البند الأول من بين بندين في جدول الأول :-

في إطار محاولاتنا لتوحيد الجهود ، نحن بحاجة للاتفاق على قضيتن منفصلتين ولكنها ذات علاقة ببعضهما البعض ، الأولي وهي العمل

على توحيد الجهود من أجل ايجاد جبهة موحدة بغرض تغيير النظام ، والثانية هي تطوير وثقل تجارب مختلف الاحزاب والمنظمات المدنية من أجل تشجيع نظام ديمقراطي يقوم على تعدد الأحزاب فيما يلي سقوط النظام ، ونحن نتعاطي مع القضية الأولي يجب دائما أن نكون متنبهين للمزالق التي تعتري هذا الطريق لجهة رغبة الاحزاب والتنظيمات السياسية ، والمنظمات المدنية لعدم المساومة والسعى لتحقيق كافة شروطها رافضة تقديم تنازلات أو الوصول الى حلول وسط ، واضعين هذه الخلفية في الاعتبار هل يمكن الوصول الى جبهة موحدة حول الهدف المشترك وهو تغيير النظام ؟ إن وجهة نظري الشخصية هي نعم رغم تلك الخلفية إلا انهم قادرون الى الوصول الى جبهة موحدة ، وبالتأكيد هو أمر يستحق المحاولة للدفع بهم للاتفاق ، لأن البديل هو الانتظار حتى حدوث التغيير بناء على عامل الحظ أو الصدفة.

إن تجربة (سدري) تعتبر تجربة مفيدة للوصول الى ذلك الهدف ، اثناء القاء خطابي وفيما تلى ذلك ، طرحت سؤالا ما اذا كان بالامكان أن تلعب سدري دوراً توحيدياً بين الإرتريين ، الذين لا يزالون منقسمين على عدة محاور ، الآن بعد مرور خمسة سنوات ، أستطيع أن اقول اننى لم أرى أي مؤشر إيجابي للاجابة على سؤال الجبهة الموحدة لتغيير النظام ، وبالتأكيد السؤال ليس مقتصرعلى سدري بل موجه ايضاً كافة المنظمات المدنية مثل - منظمة التضامن العالمي الإرتري (**EGS**)- وربما تكون هنالك منظمات مدنية أخري بذات الأهداف المماثلة لسدري والتضامن العالمي الارتري التي ربما لا اكون على علم بها. بالتأكيد الكثيرون يعتقدون مثلي كما في عام 2009م ، أن قيادات المنظمات المدنية يمتلكون الخصائص المطلوبة

مثل الالتزام ، المثابرة ، والحكمة للابحار في المياة المضطربة للواقع السياسي والاجتماعي الارتري في الوقت الحالي.

إن التجارب الحديثة اثبتت أن التنظيمات السياسية الإرترية ، وكذلك منظمات المجتمع المدني لديها النزعة تجاه الانقسامات وخلق مزيد من الكيانات ، وفي سياق الوعد الغير منجز تجاه الوحدة الوطنية فإن حالة الانقسامات التي تعتري المعارضة الإرترية تسببت في حالة من الاحباط لدى الإرتريين في كل مكان. إن المنظور التاريخي دائماً ما يساعد في تفسير ظاهرة الانقسامات ، كما ذكرت سابقاً فإنه كان هنالك بصيص من الأمل في مطلع في نهاية التسعينات وبداية الالفين ، عقب مطالبة الـ **(G15)** بالاصلاحات الديمقراطية ، مع إنشاء أحزاب جديدة منافسة للجبهة الشعبية وقد أدى ذلك الى تصاعد وتيرة الامل والتجديد ، اليوم الإرتريين بشكل عام ، واعضاء التنظيمات بشكل خاص يطالبون بوحدة التنظيمات والفصائل الارترية. ونتيجة لذك بعد سنوات من الحوارات السلحفائية بين مختلف التنظيمات والفصائل ، أخيراً ظهر التحالف الديمقراطي الإرتري ، وقد عقد مؤتمر في محاولة منه لتوسيع إطار الوحدة التي تتجاوز الاختلافات الدينية والقومية والتنظيمية ، وآخر المؤتمرات في هذا المضمار عقد في مدينة أواسا باثيوبيا ، وأنشأ المجلس الوطني ، ولازالت محاولة البحث عن الوحدة مستمرة حتى اليوم ، في الوقت ذاته فإن الحزب الديمقراطي الارتري ذو خلفية الجبهة الشعبية انضم الى جبهة التحرير الارترية - المجلس الثوري سابقاً ، وكون التنظيمان حزب الشعب الديمقراطي الإرتري ، في مسعى تجاوز حالة الانقسام والتنافس التي اصبحت سمات تاريخية ملازمة للتنيظمات الارترية .

البند الثاني : الوحدة والتعدد:-

إن التمسك بالوحدة الوطنية ضرورة مشروعة ، نجد أن البعض يساوره القلق من انه خلال سعينا الدؤوب لانجاز الوحدة الوطنية التي تعتبر شرط في مضمار النضال لتغيير النظام ، ربما بشكل غير مقصود نعيد استحداث نظام مركزي استبدادي الذي هو سبب معاناتنا الحالية ، إن هذا القلق هو قلق مشروع ولا ريب ، آخذين في الاعتبار محاولات تغيير الانظمة وما ترتب على ذلك مثل ما حدث في مصر عقب الربيع العربي ، إن الاجابة على هذا القلق المشروع تأتي من خلال اتفاقية عامة بين كافة التنظيمات والفصائل الارترية للعمل الموحد بغرض تغيير النظام ، ويمكن لهذه التنظيمات والفصائل ان تستمر كمنظمات سياسية لتكون جزء من منظومة صحية في نظام ديمقراطي يقوم على تعدد الاحزاب.

إن هذه الخطوة مطلوبة لضمان عدم عودة اى حكومة استبدادية ، ولهذا لابد ان تكون هنالك اتفاقية واضحة في هذه النقطة ، اتفاقية بهذا المضمون ربما قد تكون عاملا يساعد بعض المترددين ليكون جزء من الجبهة المتحدة التي تسعي أحداث تغيير فعال للنظام ، انه ليحدوني أمل كبير في الاحزاب المنشأة حديثاً سوف تؤدي مهمة قيادة معارضة سياسية متحدة قوية تنتصر على النظام المتجبر ، وتجعل كافة ممتلكاته وأصوله تحت تصرفها.

كما هو معروف فإن احتمالات النجاح تكمن في امكانية مواجهة التحديات المتوقعة ، واحد من هذه التحديثات هو التقارب بين النظام في إرتريا والحكومة السودانية هذه العلاقة التي وجهت ضربة موجعة للمعارضة الارترية حيث اغلقت مقراتها في الخرطوم ، وهذا اجبر كافة قوى المعارضة للتوجه الى اثيوبيا ، بما في ذلك تلك القوى

التي امتنعت لوقت طويل من التوجه لأديس ابابا . هذه الخطوة أعتبرت في نظر المراقبين البراغماتين خطوة مبررة ، ولكن في نظر أولئك الذين يلقون باللوم على (التغراي) في كثير من الأمور وينظرون اليها بريبة وتردد ، خاصة بالنظر الى طموحاتها الكبيرة في تحقيق (تغراى العظمي) تعاملوا بردود فعل سلبية تجاه توجه قوى المعارضة الى اثيوبيا وفتح مقرات لها في أديس ابابا، أن انقسام المعارضة في تعاطيها مع هذه القضية يعكس حجم التعقيدات في السياسة الارترية ، والسياسة في الاقليم بشكل عام ، وقد تعقد الأمر اكثر نتيجة لتبعات الحرب الارترية الاثيوبية (حرب بادمي) وحالة اللا حرب واللاسلم في ظل احتلال متواصل لإراضي إرترية بواسطة اثيوبيا.

البحث المستمر للمخرج:-

السؤال الحاضر دائماً هو ، ما الذي يجب فعله إذاَ ؟ الخيار المفضل بشكل عام هو المطالبة المتواصلة بتغيير نظام اسياس وتقديمه للمحاكمة على العديد من الجرائم ، وقد ظل العديد يفعلون ذلك سواء كانوا اعضاء في تنظيمات سياسية ، أو بصفاتهم الشخصية لكن دون جدوى.

جزء أساسي من الجدل حول هذا الخيار هو الخلاف حول وسائل التغيير من خلال الوسائل السليمة ام الكفاح المسلح ، بالنسبة لشعب امضى اكثر من جيلين في الكفاح المسلح ، ودفع ثمناً غالياً من دمائه وثرواته ، فإن غالبية الارتريين مترددين في قبول خيار الكفاح المسلح ، وعندما تواجه مناصري الكفاح المسلح بسؤال كيف سيحققون اهدافهم من خلال الوسائل السلمية فإن اجابتهم تأتي أولا : انهم بصدد تنظيم الجماهير في الداخل بكافة الوسائل المتاحة ، ثانياً :

فإنهم يركزون على الوسائل الدبلوماسية خاصة من خلال طلب مساعدات من دول الجوار خاصة اثيوبيا ، وحول هذه القضية بالتحديد لا يزال هنالك خلاف مستمر بين كافة فصائل وتنظيمات المعارضة الارترية ، ولم تستطع الوصول الى نتيجة حاسمة بعد ، ولهذا فإن قوى المعارضة لم تستطع التوصل الى استراتيجية دبلوماسية موحدة ، وقد حاولت العديد من المنظمات المدنية ، وبعد مدراء المواقع الارترية على الانترنيت لدفع القضية من خلال إجراء مقابلات وكتابة مقالات كل في موقعه على الانترنيت ، إن أحساسي هو الذي يدفعني للقول أن الغالبية من الارتريين تفضل الخيار السلمي ، والبعض يفضل اضافة "أن الخيار العسكري يجب أن لا يكون محرماً" . منطلقاً من فرضية أن الخيار السلمي هو الخيار المفضل لغالبية الارتريين ، فإنه سيكون على عاتق جميع الارتريين المهتمين ، العمل باصرار من أجل إيجاد استراتيجية دبلوماسية موحدة ، وجبهة تعمل على تعبئة الارتريين في الداخل ، إن الاذاعة التي بدأتها (مجموعة المنتدي - مدرخ) تعتبر مبشرة ويمكن ان تكون نواه لحملة مشتركة مثل الحملة التي بدأها (ودي فكارو) والتي يمكن ان تكون مركزاً لحملة تعبئة جماهيرية واسعة تدفع بجبهة التغيير ، ويمكن لهذه المبادرة أن تنسق مع المبادرات الأخرى ، لأن آخر ما نحتاجه هو المنافسة البغيضة بين قوى المعارضة .

جرائم الماضي ، المعالجة وإزالة الغبن :-

بصرف النظر عن الخيارات التي تم طرحها فيما سبق ، هنالك خيار آخر كسبيل للمصالحة الوطنية ، إننا نحتاج ان نكون واضحين فيما يتعلق بما هو على المحك في هذا الصدد ، إن ابحاثي الاخيرة والتي اجريتها لنشر كتابي (الأمة المجروحة) اظهرت لي انه كان هنالك

جوانب غير سارة وفظيعة في مسيرة النضال المسلح وسط الاعمال النبيلة والتضحيات البطولية . إن شعبنا بحاجة الى علاج الجراحات النفسية التي حدثت طوال فترة الكفاح المسلح ، إن الشفاء لابد أن يبدأ أولا بالاعتراف وقبول حقيقة أننا امة مكلومة ، وبالتالي نحن نحتاج اقصى درجات المساعدة الممكنة في مسار الشفاء الطويل ، ولكن كما ذكرت فإن القبول بالتشخيص هو شرط اساسي للشفاء ، وهو شرط كذلك للمصالحة الوطنية ، البعض قد يجادل قائلاً إن المطلوب هو العكس ، أى أن الشفاء يأتي كنتيجة طبيعية للمصالحة ، وهنا يبرز السؤال : هل من الممكن أن تكون هنالك مصالحة وطنية متجاوزة الجرائم التاريخية لأسياس افورقي ؟ وهل اسياس هو المذنب الوحيد ؟ بالنظر الى التعقيدات التي تحيط بهذه القضية ، فإن اغلبية الذين ناقشتهم في هذه القضية أكدوا أنه لا يمكن عملياً تقديم اسياس للعدالة إلا بعد تغيير النظام وإحلال نظام ديمقراطي ، وحكم دستوري ، وهكذا تدور القضية في حلقة مفرغة.

بعيداً عن المحاكمات عن الجرائم والشعور بالذنب ، نجد أن معظم قوى المعارضة لديها مقترحات حلول تتضمن علاجاً سياسياً يحتوى على احداث التغيير الديمقراطي واقامة حكم دستوري يقوم على قواعد القانون وحقوق الانسان كركائز اساسية للجسم الارتري العليل . بالتأكيد الغالبية سوف تتفق مع هذه الوصفة العلاجية ، ولكن غني عن القول أن نردد السؤال الذي يتبادر الى الذهن : كيف يمكن وضع هذه الوصفة العلاجية موضع التنفيذ ؟ إن الاجابة على هذا السؤال نكرر مرة أخري انه لايمكن أن يحدث تغيير مالم يكن هنالك حراك في داخل إرتريا .

يبدو واضحاً في ظل التقييد الكامل لحرية التعبير والتنظيم ، وفي ظلّ تضيق الخناق الذي تمارسه الاجهزة الأمنية وحالة الرعب التي تبثها ، فإن ظهور حركة في الداخل الارتري صعب جداً أن لم يكن المستحيل بعينه ، إن حركة - فورتو بقيادة ود علي- أظهرت أن هنالك حراك تحت السطح ، وهو حراك غير منظم لابد من السعى الى تنظيمه ، وبالمختصر فإن حراك وطني منظم في الداخل يحتاج الى تشجيع ودعم من الإرتريين في الخارج ، كيف يمكن أن يحدث ذلك هو سؤال المرحلة.

أن من المناسب في هذه المرحلة أن نذكر أن مجموعة من الشباب الاكاديمين من الذين يعتقدون أن التغيير يمكن أن يأتي من الداخل ، ليس من خلال تغيير النظام بل من خلال مخاطبة القيادة في الحكومة الإرترية والحزب الحاكم لإحداث التغيير الذاتي ، ولهذا الغرض فقد كتب هؤلاء خطاباً موجه الى كافة القيادات العليا في الدولة ، وبالتحديد الوزراء في الحكومة وقيادات الحزب في أعقاب حادية لامبيدوسا المأساوية ، الخطاب تمت كتابته بلغة دبلوماسية محترمة ، والخطاب في مضمون ينطلق من فرضية أن المخاطبين بالرسالة يؤمنون بالقيم الديمقراطية التي يؤمن بها اصحاب المبادرة ، وبالتأكيد لا يتضمن اى من القناعات الراسخة لدى المعارضة والتي تؤمن بأن اسياس متهم في جرائم خلال مرحلة الكفاح المسلح ، آخذين في الاعتبار النظرة المتفائلة لهؤلاء الاكاديمين ومحترمين حقهم في تفضيل اسياس ونظامه ، ولكن افتراضهم أن اسياس يمكن أن يتقبل أى نداء يحاول ان يصحح مساره هو السذاجة بعينها على أقل تقدير ، بالمقابل فإن ضرورة مساءلة اسياس عن الجرائم ، وتقديمه الى العدالة هي رؤية تم تناولها في العديد من الاجتماعات والمقالات في مواقع المعارضة ، وفي الآوانة الاخيرة أحد الاكاديمين - استاذ علوم

سياسية - قدم ورقة في إجتماع نظمته منظمة التضامن العالمي الارتري في العاصمة الامريكية واشنطن ، وقد تضمنت الورقة مبادرة لحشد التأييد الجماهيري لحملة المطالبة بتقديم اسياس الى العدالة.

الإرتريين في الخارج وقضية اللاجئن:-

في الوقت الذي توجد فيه العديد من المشكلات الملحة التي تواجه المعارضة الارترية في المهجر وتحتاج الى معالجة، ومشكلات تواجه الارتريين في مناطق تواجدهم في اروبا ، امريكا ، والمناطق الأخرى حيث يتواجد الارتريون ، ولكن تبادلت بعض الافكار مع عدد من المواطنين الارتريين ، طالباً رؤاهم حول كيفية الإجابة على الاسئلة التالية المتعلقة بالمشكلات التي تواجه بلادنا. وقد طرحت القضية تحت عنوان - أى المسارات تسير إرتريا - إن طرحي للسؤال ومحاولة الاجابة عليه ، أود أن اوضح بجلاء أنني لا أمثل اى حزب أو مجموعة ، كما أود أن اعلن أن المعارضة الارترية هي محل تأييدي ودعمي المخلص في محاولاتهم لإنجاز المهمة التي نذروا لها انفسهم ، وكذلك منظمات المجتمع المدني ، وفي نفس الوقت يحدوني أمل كبير أن تتجاوز كافة القوى السياسية التركة المريرة للماضي وتصبح موحدة متحلية بروح وطنية جديدة لأنقاذ الوطن. عليهم أن يفكروا بروح خلاقة ، ويعملوا في معارضة موحدة ، فقط بمثل هذه الروح ومثل هذه الوحدة يمكن أن ينتصروا على النظام الغاشم. أنها الخلاصة التي توصلت اليها خلال متابعني للمعارضة طوال عقد من الزمان وتحليلي للشواهد المتعلقة بنشاطاتهم ، صحيح أن هنالك تقدم حدث في موضوع توحيد الجهود ، ولكنه لا

يزال بعيداً عن المستوى المطلوب لتحقيق التغيير الديمقراطي في إرتريا.

المنظمات المدنية بدورها ظهرت في أمريكا ، أوربا بواسطة أفراد مخلصين الذين لعبوا ادوراً ايجابية ، ولكن واضعين في الاعتبار أن المطلوب هو تغيير النظام ولذلك على أهمية المنظمات المدنية ولكنها يجب أن لا تحل محل القوى السياسية الفعالة . يجب أن يكون هنالك اتفاق عام حيث يتكامل فيه نشاط التنظيمات السياسية والمنظمات المدنية ، فالقوى المدنية يفضل أن تكون مكملة وليس بديلاً للأحزاب السياسية ، المرء يتطلع للوقت التي فيها تقوم المنظمات المدنية بإدانة نشاط او مشروع محدد تقوم به الحكومة او المنظمات ، في الوقت الذي تستخدم فيه الأحزاب السياسية لغة دبلوماسية ولا تلجأ للإدانة او الرفض ولكنها تؤيد بصمت موقف المنظمات المدينة الرافضة ، أنه خيال يرفع الروح المعنوية ، في كل الأحوال فإن المنظمات المدنية ايضاً يتطلب أن تكون اكثر تماسكا ووحدة وأن تتم هيكلتها بشكل افضل حتى تستطيع تحقيق أهدافها . ذلك الهدف هو الذي دفعني لقبول الدعوة والمشاركة دون أى تردد في المؤتمر التأسيسي لـ (سدري) ، وبنفس الروح أيضاً شاركت في الاجتماع الذي نظمه بواسطة (التضامن العالمي الارتري) تحت شعار (صوت حكم القانون) وهو شرف أنا ممتمن كثير له.

أن مما يجدر تأكيده هو أن المنظمات المدنية تحتاج الى وضوح وتجانس في الرؤية والأهداف ، محددين بوضوح الحدود التي تميزهم عن التنظيمات والاحزاب السياسية في المعارضة من أجل تجنب سوء الفهم والصراعات التي لا لزوم لها . إن المنظمات المدنية والتنظيمات السياسية يتوقع منها أن تلعب دوراً مهما في كشف

وتعرية الفوضى والبطش التي يمارسها النظام ضد شعبنا ، كما يتوقع منهما الاسهام في حل مشكلات بعض الضحايا خاصة أولئك الذين يهربون من قبضة النظام ، وفي هذا المضمار فإن المواقع المعارضة يتوقع من أدواراً حاسمة وهي التي بدورها أيضاً مطلوب منها اتفاق عام فيما بينها حول الاهداف المشتركة وتجنب المواجهات والإتهامات المتبادلة ، إن واحد من الاهداف المشتركة الاساسية هو تعبئة العدد الكبير من اللاجئين بمختلف فئاتهم من أجل إحداث التغيير في إرتريا ، وهنا يجب الاقرار دون مواربة أن الجهد المبذول والمقدم لا يزال دون المطلوب. إن المعارضة في سعيها لتحقيق النجاح حتاج الى مضاعفة الجهود ، وتبنى وسائل خلاقة وحديثة في جذب الشباب الى صفوفها خاصة أولئك الذين هربوا من قبضة النظام ، ولتحقيق ذلك أنه من الأهمية بمكان تحليل مكونات وفئات الارتريين في المهجر.

إن الغالبية العظمي من الإرتريين في المهجر هم من الذين هربوا من قبضة النظام في العقد الأخير ، إن تفاصيل رحلتهم الاسطورية في الهروب من النظام اكبر شهادة على الروح الانسانية التي تعكس الشجاعة ، العزيمة ، المثابرة و الابداع وهى سمات تميز الإرتريين ، عدد قليل من هؤلاء الهاربين أنضموا الى تنظيم سياسي أو أكثر من تنظيم ، كما أن البعض انضم الى المنظمات المدنية ، ولكن الغالبية العظمى بقيت خارج هذه الأطر ، تسير مع التيار ومركزة اهتمامها في المشكلات اليومية للحياة ، حالمة بنسيان وتجاوز قساواه الحياة التي عاشوها في الماضي ، بل إن البعض منهم عبر عن احساسه بمرارة عن تجربته ، وبالتالي لا يرغب في تذكيره بماضيه بل يريد نسيان إرتريا بالكامل. وهؤلاء يعبرون بصراحة انهم أدوا واجبهم الوطني وعلى التنظيمات والقوى السياسية أن تتوقف عن تذكيرهم

ووعظهم عن أداء الواجب لأن ذلك بالنسبة لهم هو المنافقة المطلقة. إنهم يشعرون بالمرارة وفي مثل حالهم من حق أى شخص ان يتساءل ما اذا كان هؤلاء سوف يستعيدون ايمانهم بوطنهم ، البعض يتوقع أن مستقبل هؤلاء سيكون في البلاد التي هاجروا اليها وليس في وطنهم الذي تركوه خلفهم ، بالتأكيد هذه واحدة من الجوانب المحزنة في الواقع الارتري ، وهو ما يثير العديد من التساؤلات الحقيقية التي سوف يكون لها انعكاسات على مستقبل إرتريا.

هذا أيضاً سوف يمر :-

منذ مأساة حادية لامبيدوسا ، فإن قضية الهجرة الكثيفة للشباب من إرتريا الى الخارج ، غالباً اروبا وأمريكا اصبحت تحتاج الى اهتمام جدّي اكثر مما هو حادث الآن ، على المدى القصير يمكن مساعدة هؤلاء الشباب المحتاجين الى مساعدات عاجلة في مختلف الجوانب ، أما على المدى المتوسط او الطويل ، يمكن أن تكون هذه القضية موضع ابحاث لطلاب العلوم السياسية والاجتماعية والتاريخ ، ولكن هذه تعتبر رفاهية في الوقت الحالي لأن الذين هم في حاجة الى الاحتياجات العاجلة لا يمكنهم التأمل . خلال اجراء بحث في عام 2009-2010م ، تلقيت افادة من احد اعضاء الكنيسة الانجيلية أن حوالي اربعة الاف من هؤلاء الشباب (الذين اسميتهم لاجئ ساوا) قد انضموا الى كنيستهم ، لدى احساس أن العدد المنضم للكنيسة الانجيلية في تزايد بسبب أن الكنيسة الانجيلية لديهم الدوافع الكافية لمساعدة هؤلاء الشباب لتأسيس حياة هادفة تتضمن الدراسة ، العمل ، تأسيس أسرة ، وهم في وضع افضل لتلقى المساعدات من زملائهم في الكنيسة من وطنهم الأصل ، وتعتبر بريطانيا خير مثال في لذلك. في رأي أن المعارضة خاصة قطاع المنظمات المدنية مطلوب منها

الأهتمام بهؤلاء الارتريين بشكل جدي بقدر ما تستحقه من جدية واشراكهم في انشطتها البناءة ، إن المبدأ لابد أن يكون السعي الدؤوب لإشراك كافة الارتريين في المشاركة في القرارات التي تتعلق مصيرهم كشعب بغض النظر عن الدين او الأصل أو القومية .

عندما أفكر في مأساتنا كإرتريين في الوقت الحالي ، لا أستطيع سوى تذكر الكلمات المؤرقة لضحايا (البدون) في سيناء ، كلمات بعض الشباب الارتري اثناء التعذيب قبل عملية استخراج الكلى والاعضاء الحيوية الأخرى من اجسادهم بغرض التجارة الرائجة في شبه جزيرة سيناء إنها حوادث غير قابلة للنسيان. حتى في لحظات مواجهة الموت ، واثناء استخراج الاعضاء الحيوية من أجسامهم ولكنهم خلفوا للأجيال عباراتهم المتمسكة بالأمل (هذا أيضاً سوف يمر) . إن كل من يشكك في الروح البطولية للإرتريين في المحن يجب ان يتذكر هؤلاء الابطال المجهولين ، كلنا يجب ان نستمد الروح من هؤلاء الابطال الصغار روح تلهمنا المثابرة. نحن بحاجة الى التفكير الجاد والتركيز بوضوح فيما يمكن تلبيته من الاحتياجات الماسة لهؤلاء الشباب ، ومناقشة ما يمكن تقديمه لتخفيف معانهم وإيجاد حلول لها ، ما الذي يمكن عمله لمساعدتهم على التأقلم ، والاستمرار في الحياة ، والمساهمة في الهّم المشترك ؟ طالما إن تقديم العون والمساعدة للاجئين من الأهمية بمكان ، فإن تنظيمات المعارضة والمنظمات المدنية بحاجة للبحث عن مصادر أخرى للدعم ، مصادر رسمية وغير رسمية ، إن مجموعة العمل التي تم تأسيسها في عام 2008م تعتبر مبادرة جيّدة ، كما أن المبادرة الجيّدة التي قام بها (ودي فاكارو) يجب تطويرها الى الى حملة شعبية تسعى الى إحداث تغيير سياسي ، ومساعدة اللاجئين والنازحين في أى مكان ، ولكن الأولوية الملحة يجب ان تولى الى مأساة الإرتريين في إسرائيل وفي

سيناء المصرية حيث ترتكب الجرائم الفظيعة في حق الإرتريين ولا تزال.

الإعتراف المتبادل - الركيزة الأولي لوجود وبقاء الوطن :-

في محاولات إستشراف المستقبل لما بعد زوال النظام ، واضعين في الاعتبار المأزق الذي نعيشه كما تم توصيفه في الفصول السابقة ، يجب أن نسأل بعض الأسئلة المهمة حول واقعنا إدارته او تطويره ، ولنبدأ اولاً بمشروع الدستور لشعب متعدد الاعراق (لزاماً عليه أن يقّر الاعتراف المتبادل كمبدأ اساسي للحكم ووجود الوطن) أياً كان نوع الدستور الذي يتباه ، لا يمكن تجاهل أو القفز على هذا المبدأ مطلقاً ، ولعل في قول الباحث الكندي المعروف جيمس تالي **(James Tully)** ما يوضح ذلك بوضوح في قوله (إن سؤال عصرنا الحالي هو أياً كان نوع الدستور طالما يعترف بالمطالب المشروعة للاعراق والثقافات المتعددة بطريقة ترضي الجميع ، ويوافق عليه الكل بحرية كاملة ،هذا الشكل من الترابط الدستوري دعونا نسمية (الاعتراف المبتادل) ونسأل ما الذي يحتويه).

فيما يتعلق بهذه القضية ، نحتاج أن نسأل هل نحن مدركون لخطوط التصدع المترتبة على التعدد داخل الوطن ، واذا كنا ندرك تلك الخطوط فهل يمكن تجسيرها ، وما الذي يمكن أن تفعله التنظيمات السياسية في هذا السياق من أجل المحافظة على إرتريا موحدة أرضاً وشعباً؟ هل التعدد الديني والعرقي هو خطوط التصدع ، اذا كان كذلك فما الذي يمكن عمله لتجسير الهوة بين هذه الاختلافات ؟ ما الذي يمكن أن نتعلمه من الماضي خاصة فيما تتعلق بالانقسامات على أسس دينية ، وما هي المواد والاحكام الدستورية التي يجب أن نصر عليها لتجسير الهوة ؟ هل أياً من التنظيمات السياسية او المنظمات

المدنية الإرترية عالجت هذه القضية في ادبياتها ؟ اذا كان نعم فبأى طريقة ؟ وماذا كانت النتائج؟ أنه لا يخفى على أحد ان هنالك تعبيرات ومظاهر واضحة لخطوط التصدع ، استبعاد بعد القوميات من قسمتهم في السلطة والثروة ، إن ظهور العديد من التنظيمات السياسية في حد ذاته سواء سلباً او ايجاباً هو انعكاس واقعي لخطوط التصدع ؟ هل يمكن ادراج او استيعاب ظهور هذا العدد من التنظيمات تحت مبدأ (الوحدة في التعدد)؟

سأنطلق من فرضية ان كافة المنظمات على اختلافها بما فيها المجموعات التي ظهرت حديثاً مثل (المنتدي - مدرخ) ومثيلاتها يحملون مصلحة وطنهم وشعبهم في قلوبهم ، ويمكنهم أن يلعبوا دوراً في تجسير الهوة بين خطوط التصدع ، وأنطلق من ايماني العميق أن تجسير الهوة بين هذه الخطوط وحده كفيل بالحفاظ على إرتريا كبلد موحد أرضاً وشعبا ، إن هذا الدور لا يتوقف فقط على المنظمات بل يتجاوزه الى الافراد ، ولدينا في مبادرة (ودي فاكارو) مثال حيّ حيث استطاعت مبادرته ملامسة مشاعر أغلب الارتريين في المهجر قياساً على المشاركة الكبيرة في اللقاءات التي نظمها ، والجهود المتواصلة للترويج لخلق جبهة متحدة من أجل اسقاط النظام في اسمرا ، وهنا يجب التأكيد أن آخر ما نحتاجه هو الاتهامات المتبادلة ، والمعارك الجانبية بين تنظيمات المعارضة ، لأن المرحلة تحتاج الى كافة المجموعات موحدة من أجل تحقيق الأهداف المشتركة ، متعالين على المصالح الضيقة حزبية كانت او شخصية ، وعندما يتحقق الهدف الأساسي وهو تغيير النظام ، حينها يمكن أن نقول انه آن الآوان لظهور المئات من المدارس الفكرية ، آن الآوان للديمقراطية التي تقوم على التعدد الحزبي .

المزيد من الأسئلة لكافة الارتريين:-

1. ما هي رؤيتك حول الأوضاع والسيناريو المأساوي لمعاناة الارتريين الموضحة في الورقة ؟

2. ما الذي يجب أن يفعله الارتريون في المهجر في اعتقادك؟

3. بالنظر الى دوافع اسياس الت دعته لاختراع لمعسكر ساوا - مشروع الخدمة الوطنية - للتحكم في الشباب وبالتالي البقاء في السلطة ، هل تعتقد أن النظام يمكن أن يغيّر هذه السياسة كما يعتقد بعض الإرتريين؟

4. على ضوء أن غالبية الارتريين في الخارج فضل البقاء خارج إطار معسكر المعارضة ، وبالنظر الى أن المعارضة لم تظهر المقدرة الكافية لتغيير النظام ، او حتى لإجباره على تغيير سياساته وممارساته ، ما الذي يجب فعله الآن؟

السيناريوهات المحتملة:-

على ضوء حقيقة استمرار النظام في فعل ما يشاء بما يتعارض مع مصالح الشعب ، ضع في الاعتبار أن الشعب في هذه الحالة سوف يتنبى أحد الخيارات التالية:-

أ. الاستمرار على ما هو موجود.

ب. الاعتراف بالهزيمة والاستسلام للنظام ونسيان فكرة النضال.

ج. ايجاد شكل نضالي بديل.

لا يمكننى أن أتخيل أن أى شخص ماعدا مناصري النظام يوصي بالخيارات الأول والثاني ، فاذا كان كذلك هل تتفق معي أن السيناريو المتوقع هو الثالث؟ اذا كان ذلك هو الخيار ، فإن السؤال الذي يطرح نفسه أى شكل من اشكال النضال ، وماذا نفعل بالتنظيمات القائمة؟ بالتأكيد انه ليس مفضلاً او ممكناً علمياً الغاء التنظيمات الموجودة حالياً ، ليس مفضلاً لأن هذه التنظيمات ثروة سياسية واجتماعية جاهزة ، لها تاريخ وقد استثمر فيها الشعب الكثير من حيث الوقت والجهد ، وهو غير ممكن عملياً لأن الطبيعة الانسانية كما هو معروف لا يمكن اقناع انسان استثمر الكثير في تنظيم سياسي او منظمة مدنية بترك تنظيمه او منظمته ، بالتأكيد فذلك أمر غير بناء بالمرة ، وعلى ضوء ذلك ما الذي يجب عمله؟

الخلاصة:-

سوف اختم بإعادة التأكيد على قضيتين ، الأولى الحاجة للاتفاق على الدستور ، والأخرى قضية الجرائم والعقاب المترتب عليها. بخصوص الدستور فإن رأي معروف بشكل عام ، وهو أنني أومن بقوة مثل ايمان (ود علي) ورفاقه في في حادثة (فورتو) بأن دستور عام 1997م يجب أن يستخدم كقاعدة مشتركة لتغيير النظام ، ولكن يمكن لقوى التغيير في اتفاقها على موضوع الدستور أن تقوم بتعديله أو تبني دستور جديد ، أما بخصوص القضية الأخرى ، ربما البعض او معظم الارتريين يبدو مصرين على ضرورة معاقبة كل القيادات الارترية التي إرتكبت جرائم ، بينما يؤمن البعض بالصفح والمسامحة من أجل انجاح المصالحة الوطنية والسلام . والرأى الاخير ينطلق انه من الضرورة أحيانا من أجل تحقيق المصالحة لابد من اعتماد مبدأ (عفا الله عما سلف) والعفو عن كافة الجرائم التي

ارتكبت في فترة الكفاح المسلح . إن الارتريين الذين كانوا ضحايا لقيادات جبهة التحرير او الجبهة الشعبية خلال حقبة الكفاح المسلح ، أو اقاربهم ربما يحتاجون الى جهود كبيرة لإقناعهم بهذا المبدأ حتى من أجل المصالحة الوحدة الوطنية ، أنها فعلا جرعة مريرة يصعب تقبلها ، ولكن في ذات الوقت علينا انا نفكر بجّد ، ونبحث عن البدائل ، لابد من التفكير في المصلحة العليا ، نحتاج الى تكثيف وتعميق الحوار الوطني ، إن من محاسن الصدف أن هذه القضية من صميم تخصصي ، وقد سبق وأجريت بحوثاً في مجال الجرائم والعقوبات فيما يتعلق ببعض الدول الأفريقية من بينها جنوب أفريقيا ، يوغندا ، سيراليون وليبريا.

القضية هنا انه يبدو ان هنالك ضرورتان متعارضان ، الاولي ضرورة اقرار المصالحة والسلام ، والثانية ضرورة إقرار العدالة ، فالعدالة تقتضي احضار المجرميين لمواجهة العدالة ، واقرار العقوبات التي تتناسب والجرائم التي ارتكبوها ، وعادة الضحايا أو اقاربهم من الطبيعي أن يطالبوا بتقديم مرتكبي الجرائم الى العدالة ، هذا طبيعي ويجب أن يكون متوقعاً قي حالنا كإرتريين. ولكن بالمقابل في مواجهة النزاعات التي لا نهاية لها في بعض الدول الافريقية ، او الاستبداد الذي لا نهاية له كما هو في حالنا في إرتريا ، ربما نواجه بضرورة تاريخية للتسوية .

إن جنوب افريقيا تجاوزت ذلك من خلال انشاء مفوضية الحقيقة والمصالحة ، وتم تخيير مرتكبي الجرائم أن يقفوا أمام المفوضية ويعترفوا بما ارتكبوه ويسألوا الضحايا أو اقاربهم الصفح و العفو، أما أولئك الذين رفضوا المثول أمام المفوضية فقد تمت محاكمتهم من خلال المحاكم ونالوا العقوبات التي تتناسب وجرائمهم.

في ظل الظروف الحالية لنا نحن كإرتريين في معسكر المعارضة الارترية يبدو انه لا يمكننا تطبيق نموذج جنوب افريقيا لمعالجة قضايا الجرائم والعقوبات ، لسبب اساسي وهو انه لتطبيق هذا النموذج يجب ان تكون هنالك حكومة تنشئ المفوضية وتفوضها الاختصاص والصلاحية للتعامل مع هذه القضايا ، بالتأكيد ليس لدينا هذه الحكومة إلا اذا وافق اسياس على ذلك ، على قاعدة ضمان العفو عن جرائمه وجرائم كل الذين ارتكبوا جرائم في الماضي ، وبالطبع فإن العديد في معسكر المعارضة يرفضون العفو عن جرائم الماضي.

واخيراً ، لدينا المخزون الاحتياطي ، وهو ثروتنا الاجتماعية الحديثة منها والتقليدية ، الحديثة تضم الادباء والمهنيين ، الذين لم يأخذوا مكانتهم التي يستحقونها خلال مرحلة النضال ، وفي الجانب التقليدي لدينا الشيوخ الذين أورثهم العمر الحكمة والتجربة والذين من بينهم ايضاً الادباء والمهنيين ، إن أحياء هذا المخزون الاحتياطي التقليدي هو شئ قّيم ، وهذا الاحياء يمكن أن يكون دافعه الضرورة الملحة حالياً للمصالحة وجبر الأضرار . أننا نحتاج بشكل جدي العمل على تحديد قائمة من الشيوخ الارتريين تتضمن قيادات مدنية ودينية من الارتريين في المهجر ، وكذلك من الأدباء والمهنيين ، هذه القائمة ايضاً يجب ان تضمن قيادات في التنظيمات السياسية و المنظمات المدنية ، بالتأكيد فإن كل احد من هؤلاء لديه علاقات واتصالات بالداخل يستطيع أن يتواصل معهم بشكل سري من أجل التعبئة في هذه المرحلة .

إن كافة الملاحظات والمقترحات التي أوردتها في هذه الورقة تنطلق من الاحساس العميق بخطورة المرحلة والحاجة الملحة لإيجاد الحلول ، ولدى إيمان لا يتزعزع انه لابد من التعامل مع هذه القضايا بجدية

اذا اردنا لوطننا وشعبنا البقاء ، أتمنى صادقاً ان تجد هذه القضايا الاهتمام الكافي الذي تستحقه ، إن أحساسي بخطورة المرحلة مرتبط بالخطر الكبير الذي يهدد بقاء أمة كانت واعدة ، أنني اتوجه بنداء خاص الى جيل الألفية والذي وقبله ، الذين كانوا في عمر المراهقة عندما ولدت أمتنا من جمر الكفاح المسلح ، اما نحن الشيوخ نبقى بالكاد مراقبين للوضع في الوقت الذي تتأكل فيه امتنا تدريجياً ، فهل تكون أنت منقذاً لها.